Sporting Clays

*Expert techniques for
every kind of clays course*

Michael Pearce

STACKPOLE
BOOKS

Published by
STACKPOLE BOOKS
Cameron and Kelker Streets
P.O. Box 1831
Harrisburg, PA 17105

Printed in the United States of America

10 9 8 7 6 5 4 3 2 1

First edition

Cover design and illustration by Caroline Miller

Library of Congress Cataloging-in-Publication Data

Pearce, Michael, 1958–
    Sporting clays: expert techniques for every kind of clays course
    Michael Pearce. — 1st ed.
        p.   cm.
    ISBN 0–8117–1914–6
    1. Trapshooting. I. Title.
GV1181.P43   1991
797.313—dc20   91–8655
                                                                      CIP

This book is dedicated to the men and women who have worked hard to bring sporting clays from virtual obscurity to the popularity it holds both now and in the future.

I would also like to dedicate this book to those who are actively fighting to protect the shooting sports from those who wish to close them. Without them America would surely lose its treasures of gun ownership, hunting, and target shooting in the near future. I encourage all readers to join them in this critical fight.

CONTENTS

ACKNOWLEDGMENTS

It would simply be impossible to thank all who have helped in the research and completion of this book. It was a project that was made much easier and much more enjoyable thanks to those listed below and others too numerous to mention.

First, of course, comes my wife, Kathy, and children, Lindsey and Jerrod. I thank them and love them for their support. I also apologize for the long hours that this project entailed.

I would also like to thank Gordon Philip, Gary Norris, Bob Brister, Sue King, Tim Murphy, Barbara Murphy, W. R. and Betty Murfin, Mark and Nancy Moxley, Jeff and Justin Graves, Bob Davis, Pam Webster, Kevin Howard, Mike Hampton, Larry Cero, and those whose names appear randomly throughout the book.

I would also like to express my appreciation to the staff at Stackpole Books, particularly Mary McGinnis and Judith Schnell. If there is a better staff to work with, I have not found it.

Most importantly, I'd like to thank Michael Murphy, a man whose talents and knowledge of sporting clays are overshadowed only by his excellence as a friend, and who sacrificed countless hours to assist me with this book. Simply put, I could not have done it without him. It is as much his accomplishment as it is mine. Thanks, Mike.

INTRODUCTION

As I write this it's the summer of 1990, but it seems like only a few weeks ago that I joined four gunners for an afternoon stroll in the Missouri hardwoods in the autumn of 1987. I doubt I'll ever forget the fiery reds, blazing yellows, and bright oranges of the changing foliage . . . nor the intensity of the smiles that we wore.

I was on assignment for *The Wall Street Journal*, working on an article about what some were saying was the biggest thing to hit the American shooting scene since the invention of smokeless powder—sporting clays.

On that particular trip I was a plain daisy surrounded by roses. My companions included A. J. "Smoker" Smith, a British gentleman and past world champion who is still unquestionably the number-one name in the sport, and a pair of other world-class shooters. Also in the group was Bob Davis, president of United States Sporting Clays Association.

I, on the other hand, was and still am a commoner, a typical American wing shooter. Granted I could hold my own in the quail coverts and pheasant fields of my native Kansas, but I was utterly in awe of my companions. As I recall, my score was about half of what Smith pulled off.

This all took place a relatively short time ago, but a lot has changed since then. The sport has been growing at a surprising rate, and no doubt will continue to grow. It seemed as though the extremely avid and affluent clay-target shooters were the first to pick up on sporting clays. Now it appears that my own kind—the typical, middle-class hunter who values his bird dogs more than his own well-being—is also turning on to the sport. This book is designed to help such shooters, though there's something in it for all levels. Though I am far from the class of gunners who introduced me to the sport that warm, October afternoon, I've tried to gather information from top-notch shooters like them to make this book as helpful as possible. The information should stretch beyond the clays course and into the hunting fields as well.

Please remember, however, that simply reading about the subject can't make a good shot out of a poor one. Good shooting—be it at winged or clay targets—is something that's achieved through experience. I hope the following information will make the learning process easier and more enjoyable.

Above all else, remember to shoot safely and have fun.

A HISTORY OF THE SPORT

There are some beginnings for which we know an exact date. Though we may not remember it now, there was an exact time that we each began shooting. It appears that the origin of sporting clays, however, was more of an evolution than an actual birth.

According to Britain's A. J. Smith, the sport came into being in the early part of this century. For decades it grew slowly, but that's since changed. "It has just been within about the last ten years that it has really taken off," says Smith. "Now for every trap and skeet shooter in England there are probably five sporting clays shooters." In 1987 Smith estimated that there were probably fifty sporting clays shoots every weekend and some had as many as five hundred entrants.

It's surprising that in the United States, a country with fifteen to twenty million hunters, the sport was so slow to catch on. But just because formal sporting clays didn't reach America until the mid-1980s doesn't mean that the concept was totally foreign to U.S. shooters. Many shooting clubs and shooting preserves have had special setups for decades. Often it was little more than a "crazy quail" setup, where hunters could practice on targets that tried to duplicate the many angles and challenges of gunning for bobwhites.

A.J. "Smoker" Smith, English gentleman and former world champion, greatly helped bring sporting clays to America.

Some establishments even went to the trouble of having several stations modeled after a variety of game and shooting conditions. The Campfire Club of New York had a "Hunter's Clays" course for decades.

Many avid hunters report that for years they'd used a portable thrower to practice up on their wing shooting. In our teens, my brother and I would take an old Trius target thrower to our grandfather's pasture on Sunday afternoons.

The trick was to make things as realistic and challenging as possible. Shotguns had to be on safe and held on a normal hunting position. Targets were thrown at random rather than called for, and the flight and number of "birds" were left up to the person working the trap.

A typical sequence would be for one of us to have his back to the trap while the other adjusted its direction and angle. The sound of the machine was the "flush." Sometimes there would be a single target flying high like a dove, and other times there would be a trio of low-flying "quail" that took some quick shooting to hit before they were safe on the ground.

Other hunters report having set a similar trap on a high pond, dam, or cliff to practice pass shooting at high-flying birds. Target throwers were also placed in the woods to duplicate the situations faced by a ruffed grouse hunter.

Though there is a very tiny bit of controversy about how sporting clays got its formal start in America, we can thank the Houston, Texas, area for getting the ball rolling. Bob Brister, a well-known outdoor writer for the *Houston Chronicle* and *Field & Stream* magazine, got his first taste of the sport on a trip to England in the early 1980s. The articles that he did on the "shooting sport for hunters" stirred up a great deal of interest.

Orvis was quick to incorporate the idea into its local shooting school, and the first clays tournament in America took place in 1983. According to Brister, that first shoot drew gunners from seven states. He, like many people, says he was surprised at the instant popularity. The popularity of sporting clays would continue to surprise a lot of people. It grew faster than even the wildest dreams of those who've helped get it started in America.

It was in May 1985 that the United States Sporting Clays Association (USSCA) was founded by a small group of influential Houston shooters. Bob Davis eventually took over the role of president of the organization. "We made our formal announcement at the Shooting, Hunting, and Outdoor Trade [SHOT] Show in January of 1986," recalls Davis. "We originally had reserved a room for 15 people, but we had to move it to a room for 150. The response was phenomenal!"

At that time there was but a pair of affiliated sporting clays courses in the nation. By the time I shot with Davis and company in October 1987, that number had grown to fifty-two affiliates. The number of tournaments had increased from none at the beginning of 1986 to twenty a year in 1987. Those who were promoting the sport predicted that it would continue to grow at a similar rate—and it did.

In 1989 a second organization, National Sporting Clays Association (NSCA), was formed by the same people who ran the National

One of the basics of sporting clays is getting out and having a good time in the outdoors. It's never a bad day as long as you're having fun; high scores are secondary.

Skeet Shooting Association in San Antonio. Yes, there is and probably will continue to be a little bit of competition between the two groups. But as the old saying goes, "a little competition can be good for business."

In the summer of 1990 there were an estimated three hundred to five hundred or more sporting clays courses scattered all across America. The fact that we don't know exactly how many courses there are spells one of the most exciting changes in the sport.

In its American infancy, sporting clays courses were usually synonymous with posh shooting clubs. Membership and costs per round weren't cheap, and a lot of shooters simply couldn't afford the sport. There are a good number of clays courses that are tailor-made for the corporate CEO who travels from his suburban home in a Mercedes. Luckily there are a growing number of courses designed for the pickup-driving, quail-hunting, average American as well. From huge New York

City to tiny Cimarron, Kansas, there are sporting clays courses for almost everyone.

Surely the growth will continue. The coming decade will probably see a huge rise in the number of small, "grass roots" courses. Though often not affiliated with either the USSCA or the NSCA, they are an important part of the future of sporting clays, and what's good for sporting clays is good for American shooting in general.

We all know of the ongoing and escalating attack firearms and hunting are under in America. Sporting clays is and will continue to be one of the top examples of what is good about shooting.

As the sport continues to expand, it's being taken up by more than just the traditional shooter. It's a sport for men *and* women of all ages. (See chapter 7, which is devoted to the ease and benefits of getting women and young shooters involved in the sport.) There's no question that having women involved in shooting sports has a definite calming effect on the American public.

Those of us who are already addicted to the sport should introduce a variety of friends and relatives to the charms of shooting. The intro-

A gunner enjoying the fastest growing sport in America.

duction of nonshooters is of great importance. Hand someone a Remington 11-87 or a Beretta 303 and let him break a few targets, and he'll suddenly realize that all semiautomatic guns aren't bad. A good round of clays will also give a nonhunter at least a small taste of why many of us crave following a good dog through the uplands.

Likewise, when we take our young children along to watch, why not ask them to invite a friend? We need to let the eight- and ten-year-olds see that there's more to shooting than what they see on television.

How far will the sport go? Will it ever rival trap and skeet in America as it does in some countries? Only time will tell.

---2---

THE BASICS

For decades American gunners had but two paths to follow when they headed out with a shotgun. One path led to either a trap or a skeet field for clay target shooting, both of which are of low cost and allow for as much shooting as the gunner can stand or afford. The other path meandered through the uplands and marshes of the countryside. Ours is a nation blessed with a wide variety of hunting. Whether for ducks or doves, quail or cottontails, shooters could enjoy an outdoor experience with both two- and four-legged creatures. Every day, every point, flush and retrieve are always varied. Hunters who were both skilled and lucky might carry the makings for a fine meal home along with their memories.

But as with all roads, both target shooting and hunting have a few potholes. Trap and skeet are sports of repetition. All ranges are basically alike—shooting trap in Alabama is essentially the same as shooting trap in Alaska. Some shooters find little excitement in trap and/or skeet.

Trap and skeet can also be intimidating to a beginner. Both are sports where near perfection is expected. Shooters are *supposed* to be able to toe the line and break at least 90 to 95 percent of the targets.

Personally, I've never felt comfortable displaying my lack of prowess before a tight-knit group that's disappointed by anything less than 100 percent.

At the same time, hunting isn't what it was a few years ago. There are still areas with lots of game, but it's getting tougher and tougher for many shooters to gain access, as coverts are often several hours' drive from metropolitan areas.

Hunting is also restricted by seasons. In many states, bird hunters have but three or four months in which to enjoy their sport. And a hunt can take up a lot of time, including hours or days spent lining up hunting spots and making travel arrangements. For some there's no such thing as a quick hunt.

For others, hunting may simply be too physically demanding. Someone who spends his days saddled up to a desk might find little joy in dragging an out-of-shape body through the brush and brambles of the uplands. And some of us may have reached that point in our lives when the years have reduced our endurance to but a fraction of what it once was. The short legs of a young hunter might also be a handicap. Starting a gunner with an experience that's physically punishing is a great way to turn him or her off to hunting for life.

Because of the wide differences between hunting and the target sports, there was little enthusiastic crossover. Sure, many people did both, but most were quick to point out that they were basically committed to one or the other.

With the emergence of sporting clays, American shooters were offered a third path—one that bisects the roads of both hunting and target shooting. Sporting clays resembles each in a way, yet at the same time it is unique. The basic equipment is essentially the same, and as in trap and skeet, sporting clays gunners take shots at clay targets that are thrown by sophisticated throwers. But that's where the similarities end.

Those who lay out sporting clays courses are quick to point out that they're trying to copy the experience of hunting. The outdoor setting is basically the same, but again there are some major differences, both positive and negative, when compared with wing shooting.

In its early days, sporting clays was often called "golfing with a

Sporting clays is a great family sport. This father/son pair, Jeff and Justin Graves of Kansas, has enjoyed many hours together on clays courses. It's important to introduce the sport to young people—they're the future of shooting and hunting in America.

shotgun." I assume that was because a clays course consists of a variety of stations. The exact number will vary from course to course and from day to day. Some small courses may be made of five stations, while others may incorporate as many as fifteen or twenty. The average is probably between five and ten stations.

Like the different holes on a golf course, each station is unique and offers the shooter a different type of challenge. Depending on the lay of the land, most stations are within easy walking distance from each other while still being out of sight. That gentle walk seems to be an important part of the sport. It's a relaxing time, when the shooter can simply enjoy being outdoors much more than he could on a trap or skeet field.

The isolation of the stations gives the shooter and his group at least a little privacy. There are no big crowds of strangers that can make many shooters self-conscious.

And there is no worrying about a missed bird. In sporting clays *everybody* misses some birds. A good course will have stations that almost no one can master *and* stations where even a struggling shooter can expect to break half of the birds.

The only true gauge of perfection is in the mind of the shooter. In sporting clays pure enjoyment is much more important than numbers. Sure, scores are kept, but most gunners are more worried about how their score compares with their own record rather than with that of the shooter beside them.

Unfortunately, there are aspects of hunting that sporting clays can never duplicate. There are no breathtaking points by dogs that are more a part of the family than some in-laws. There is also the lack of the unexpected that comes with hunting game, which has a mind of its own.

But unlike the other target sports, sporting clays provides a wide variety of situations, and most courses try to make the shots as realistic as possible. For example, there's usually a rule that the gun may not be mounted until the target is in sight. Most courses also require that the butt of the shotgun be clearly visible below the shooter's armpit.

Generally, each station on a course is modeled after a different hunting situation. Almost every angle imaginable is used. To add further challenge, sporting clays courses can use four or more different sizes of targets. Each variety is similar to a different type of wild-game situation with its own personality and problems.

TARGETS

Most shooters are familiar with the standard-size targets, but few have experienced the challenge of shooting minis until they've tried sporting clays. Roughly the size of a snuff can, a mini can accelerate rapidly but, because of its light weight, can slow down just as rapidly. Its small size can also make it appear farther away than it really is. No bigger than a hummingbird, a mini calls for a good, dense pattern.

Many courses also use a target size that's between the standard and the mini. Appropriately called the "midi," it's an extremely fast target that can be deceiving for those who are used to staring at standard targets.

No course would be complete without a station throwing "rabbit" targets, which are bounced and rolled along the ground to imitate supercharged cottontails. They are without a doubt among the most popular targets in the sport.

Battues have been called many, many things, most of which can't be printed. Size-wise they have about the same diameter as a standard but are not much thicker than a cookie. Battues are both fast and unpredictable. Their flight shows more irregularity than any other clay target, as they often bank from side to side.

DOUBLES

Not only can a clays course use a variety of target sizes, it can also throw a variety of doubles. The challenge of a pair of targets of different sizes flying at various angles really helps put the "sporting" into sporting clays.

In simple terms, "simultaneous doubles" are a pair of targets thrown at the same time. Sometimes one will barely trail another. Other times simultaneous doubles will fly from opposite ends of the shooting field, and the shooter must quickly reverse his gun swing after the first target is broken.

With "doubles on report," the second target is launched when the shooter pulls the trigger on the first target. Again, the targets can take similar paths or fly at radically different angles.

STATIONS

As mentioned earlier, every sporting clays station is unique. In addition to target size and doubles, courses can mix in an endless variety of angles and speeds. Most sporting clays traps can easily be adjusted to throw whatever the course designer desires.

In the hands of a good designer, traps and targets can simulate anything imaginable. The first station I ever shot had "mallards" coming high and from the left. I watched in amazement as the targets passed overhead before banking and then falling among the decoys in the small pond in front of me.

This shooter has broken one of a pair of doubles and is swinging through to try the other. Simultaneous doubles are common on nearly all sporting clays ranges.

Traps can be adjusted so that the targets follow a narrow path through dense brush, giving the shooter a brief glimpse of the target in the open.

A little bit of deception can go a long way toward keeping things challenging. A target that looks like it's flying straight away may actually be dropping . . . or rising.

A course may also change a station from day to day to mix up veteran shooters. It's a lot easier to do than it sounds. "All you have to do is to move the shooting station a few feet and it's a whole new game," says Gordon Philip, a noted course designer and sporting clays expert from Kansas City. "You can also vary the angle and the speed of the target with some minor adjustments to the thrower."

Luckily for shooters, courses usually can't pull such changes during a day's shoot. Unlike a corn-stubble rooster pheasant or a pine-timber quail, clay targets give the shooter the advantage of knowing exactly where and when they will fly.

Each gunner shoots the same sequence at a station, letting shooters plan their strategy while they wait in line. Those who don't have the benefit of watching another gunner (like the first shooter of the day) can call for and watch a practice target.

Sounds a lot easier than hunting, doesn't it? But like all things, sporting clays has a way of averaging itself out. Some of the target angles are all but foreign to most shooters.

Most upland and waterfowl shots are at rising or level-flying game. Most sporting clays courses feature at least one station where the hunter has to contend with a rapidly falling target. Challenging isn't a strong word for it—until you've had some practice.

There's also the little matter of target speed. During my first trip through a sporting clays course, I couldn't wait to get to the "crossing quail" station. "Piece of cake," I thought. "I've been shooting quail well for years. It seldom takes two shells per bird, even in the timber. This open-pasture shot will be a good way to get my score back up."

I stepped to the station, called to watch a practice pair, and my eyes nearly popped out of my head. The target was a crossing midi that was really moving. My first shot was a good four feet behind the target. A bobwhite would have to be riding in a game bag in a pickup on the interstate to be traveling that fast!

A friend standing behind me said, "It wouldn't be any fun if we hit them all." "I'll never know," I answered.

Many sporting clays courses like to incorporate local, specialized hunting shots. Here in Kansas, high, fast, incoming targets are often compared to the sport of pass shooting prairie chickens. Courses with a timbered creekbottom may try to duplicate a pair of wood ducks winding their way through the treetops. Though every course and station is unique, the following are a few themes common to most sporting clays fields:

Springing teal is one of the most popular stations in the sport because it's both challenging and easy to set up. Usually springing teal will be a simultaneous pair that's thrown nearly vertically. Most times you'd swear the targets are jet-propelled!

Decoying ducks is a fun station that often has the shooter in a duck blind, or sometimes a boat, looking out over a pond that might be covered with decoys. Generally, two targets come in high, pass in front of the blind, and then drop into the water. Getting the first target usually isn't too tough, but the second . . .

Rabbit is a station featuring a specially made target that's rolled and bounced on the ground. This station usually calls for a crossing shot, which has the shooter at the mercy of the ground—one unexpected bump and the shot will be below the high-bounding bunny.

Fur and feather combines the best of both worlds. First a rabbit target is thrown, followed by a flushing bird on report. In most cases the bird will travel in the same direction as the rabbit. More challenging setups will have the flying target angling across in the opposite direction or rising straight up.

Driven pheasant is a common station even though most Americans walk up rather than pass shoot their pheasants. This station is designed to duplicate the big drives of England and Europe. Courses often use a tower-mounted trap to throw high, incoming, and very fast targets.

Wood pigeon is another station based on a European sport. Here, shooters try to hit fast targets as they zip over a canopy of treetops.

Grouse is a station nearly always featuring targets that are rocketing through heavy timber. The timing of the shot can be as big a challenge as swinging fast enough to keep up with the target.

Woodcock is a station that, like the bird it's named after, tends to be located in dense underbrush. True woodcock stations feature targets that use deceptive angles and brush rather than speed to challenge the shooter.

---- 3 ----

COURSES

Upon finishing a frustrating morning of shooting at the famed Broadmoor Shooting Grounds in Colorado Springs, one shooter was heard to jokingly say, "You know, if I had just two shells in my gun and they lined up Saddam Hussein, Muammar Gaddafi, and [course designer] Gordon Philip in front of me, I'd have to shoot that buzzard Philip—*twice!*"

Later that day I related the story to my friend Gordon. He chuckled, smiled, and said, "Well, it looks like I did my job." He had—the course was sporting (i.e. frustrating) yet fun.

THE COMMERCIAL SPORTING CLAYS COURSE

A successful course doesn't come about by accident. Many shooters don't realize the amount of work and planning it takes to install a sporting clays course. And frequently the difference between an average and an outstanding sporting clays course is defined by the imagination of the course designer.

A lot also depends on the terrain. On America's prairies it's often simply a matter of scattering a few throwers around. But if the property is covered with trees or swamps, half the battle can be building a path to potential trap locations.

Most courses try to utilize natural terrain when installing stations. This one features a decoying duck station over a small lake. The targets come in high, then quickly drop into the water like a pair of mallards.

"Actually, all you need is a piece of land," says Philip. "You can put a sporting clays course on any kind of land—flat, mountainous, desert, or swampland."

The first step, according to the man who's put in up to sixty courses a year, is simply getting a road or path to work from. "You want to retain that land's natural terrain, but you want to make everything convenient to the shooters," explains Philip. "You don't want them having to struggle to get around. You don't want any obstacle that could result in a shooter's getting hurt."

In fact, it's the safety of the shooters and course workers that rates first and foremost with a course designer. "It can be a real worry; it can get pretty complicated, especially on courses with a lot of stations," says Philip. "You not only have to worry about where the guns are shooting, you also have to consider where the shot's going to fall and where the targets, both whole and broken, are going to fall."

It's for those reasons that a fair amount of ground is needed for a sporting clays course. "Even though you can set up a course on a trail that only takes a few minutes to walk, I'd say it usually takes about forty acres to put in a sporting clays course," states Michael Murphy, another popular course designer. "It's imperative that you have the shot and targets falling out away from the shooters. It's also important that all of the shot be contained on the same property. You can't have pellets raining down on the neighbors."

"We also have to consider if we can have all the stations going at once, safety-wise," adds Murphy. "That means protecting the trappers and spectators as well as the shooters."

One key, according to Philip and Murphy, is to take full advantage of the natural landscape. "With today's throwers you could basically set up a course with all of the popular angles and shots just about anywhere," says Murphy. "But most good designers like to make things as realistic as possible. If a course has thick timber, you can set up a grouse station in the big trees and then a quail station out near the edge. A nearby hill could be used to launch the driven pheasant targets."

Murphy also says he prefers to use the natural surroundings to hide and protect the target throwers. "It seems to be much more realistic when the shooter can't see the target thrower. Sometimes you can use a hill or dip in the landscape. Other times you may have to create your own protection. I still like to keep it natural—shot-proof but natural."

Some course designers use rocks, firewood, or huge, round hay bales to protect open-country throwers. Others may use thick plywood and disguise it with natural vegetation or camouflage netting.

Not only do course designers try to fit the type of target to the terrain, but they also have to fit target throwers to the desired shots.

Sometimes distance or reloading speeds can be crucial to the success of a station.

For many smaller courses it all boils down to the bottom line—dollars. Even the cheapest sporting clays traps can get expensive when you're buying ten of them. The difference in cost between specialty

Many of the best sporting clays courses are located in the prettiest parts of America. This course in the Rocky Mountains is at the Broadmoor Hotel near Colorado Springs.

and standard targets often sees smaller courses throwing mostly standards with a single rabbit station.

Yet some of the biggest problems facing a new sporting clays course, and even many that have been in existence for several years, lie in paperwork. According to Gordon Philip, "The absolute first thing

You don't need tree-filled and hilly country to have an excellent clays course. This one near Houston is on a broad flat and uses a variety of towers to throw high-flying targets.

you have to do is get the proper zoning and permits. You don't want to put a lot of time and money into a course, then not be able to legally open it."

There's sometimes a public-relations problem as well. More than one homeowner has objected to the distant sound of gunfire coming from a sporting clays range. Appeasing neighboring property owners before a clays course is installed can sometimes take some doing.

And it's a hassle that can recur. Sporting clays lost one of its finest courses when locals banded together to shut down the course at Game Hill Hunting Club near Kansas City.

There's also the little matter of finding and affording insurance for a clays course. With America being gun-phobic and lawsuit hungry, proper coverage doesn't come cheaply or easily.

When you consider all of the costs—land, throwers, course help, targets, and insurance—it's no wonder sporting clays is the most expensive shotgun target sport in the nation. But as the old saying goes, "You usually get what you pay for."

THROW YOUR OWN TARGETS

In some ways sporting clays can have a rather cruel effect on a person. It's often addictive, but for many it's not easily obtainable—at least not in the frequency that they'd desire.

For many middle-class shooters, course dues are a little too steep to allow shooting two or three times a week. Others, like me, also have a problem of location. My nearest course is an hour away. There's no such thing as shooting a round on the spur of the moment or as a way to kill an hour or two.

These are but a few of the reasons why more and more shooters are beginning to throw their own sporting clays targets. Think about it—you can shoot whenever you want without having to wait in line or pay regular course fees, and you can shoot exactly *what* you want. If you need a little practice on springing teal, take a case of targets and a few boxes of ammo and hit it until you get it right.

Having a few buddies chip in for target throwers can make it a fairly inexpensive proposition when you consider how long a good trap will last. A few hundred dollars from eight to ten people could buy several manual-cock, manual-load throwers.

As with a professional course designer, your only basic limitation would be your imagination. You could effectively double up on stations to save money. For example, you could shoot a right crossing pair from a trap, then move to the other side to take left crossing shots. Likewise, all that it would take to convert a high incoming to a high going-away shot would simply be turning around and facing the other way.

In fact, I've talked to a number of shooters who are setting up an entire course with one portable thrower. With the aid of a truck or four-wheel ATV with trailer, they're toting the thrower as they travel from station to station. If the station is already laid out, it only takes an

A trio of hunters practicing in a pasture. More and more clays shooters are throwing their own targets. Safety is the key.

extra minute to set up the thrower and be in business, especially with a portable thrower that has a seat and doesn't require staking.

Innovative shooters can set up a variety of stations without having to severely move the thrower. As I write this there's a Quickfire II battery-operated thrower that's haunting me from my garage. With a Hunter's Pointe rabbit arm bolted to the frame, the adjustable trap can throw just about anything my heart could desire.

Not more than a few miles from my house is a ridge that will allow me to set up an entire course by merely pivoting the thrower to toss or roll targets in different directions. By moving my shooting position from side to side on the top of the hill, on the slope, and in the valley below, I can easily shoot nine different stations.

Possible shots include the popular springing teal, fur and feather, driven pheasant incoming, driven pheasant going away, decoying ducks (falling targets), and the regular crossing and quartering shots. And I could easily shoot a round of fifty targets in far less than two hours.

Granted, such an all-in-one setup may lack some of the realism of a good sporting clays course with its varied habitats, but it's convenient and makes for great practice for both trips to affiliated courses and bird hunts. With a few partners involved, the price of the Quickfire II seems more than reasonable.

As with a commercial course, safety for the shooters and trap operators is the ultimate concern. Luckily it's one that is easily taken care of. Those who have walk-through courses can simply set up so that every target and shot flies away from the core area where all of the walking and shooting takes place. It's also safer to have just one station operating at a time. With every spectator standing behind the shooter, the chances of an accidental shooting should be nil as long as safe gun handling is practiced.

An inexpensive yet effective threshold can be made at each station to keep shooters from taking shots too far to the left or right, or above. Natural obstacles such as trees can have the same trap-protecting effect in many places.

Still, it's always a good idea to have some sort of wall to protect the trapper from an errant shot from a station. Many times the lay of the land will accomplish it. The break in the hill where I shoot my mini-course does a great job of keeping the trapper out of sight and danger.

Big, round bales of hay and sheets of thick plywood can be set up as a safeguard as well. No matter what you use, make absolutely sure there's no way a stray pellet or target piece will be able to reach the person operating the trap.

There's no substitute for good old-fashioned common sense when it comes to safety. Those who pay attention to every detail and follow the general rules of sporting clays safety should never have an accident. There could be no possible excuse for it.

---------------------------------- 4 ----------------------------------

SHOOTING

One of the most interesting aspects of attending a big sporting clays shoot is simply getting the chance to watch other people shoot. At a big tournament, like the 1990 USSCA National Championship in Colorado Springs, you can see a little bit of everything.

For example, I observed one European shooter standing as straight as a flagpole, with his legs tightly together from thigh to heel. An American shooter, on the other hand, stood with his feet far apart and his torso twisted way around as he leaned back with his left shoulder far lower than his right. His shooting wasn't overly impressive, but I was amazed that he could keep from falling over and eventually return to a normal posture.

STANCE

It's not odd that few shooters share the exact same stance. After all, we're all built differently. But I did see some amazing similarities among the truly great shooters. From California's Dan Carlisle to England's A. J. Smith and John Bidwell, the expert shooters all start with a very simple and comfortable stance. This stance requires little movement, what movement there is coming smoothly and naturally. It doesn't take a lot of time to get ready, and it no doubt would work as well in the pheasant fields of South Dakota as on the clays courses.

According to my friend and noted shooting instructor Michael Murphy, they use a stance that's so natural and simple because, as with all things, the less complicated it is, the less there is that can go wrong. The first step to learning a good shooting stance, he says, is simply to watch a few other shooters shoot the station, or at least to pay careful attention to a practice bird. "The first thing is to watch the targets and decide where you want to break the target," coaches Murphy. "I don't mean where other shooters are breaking the target; I mean where you, the shooter, want to make the shot. Some people are naturally quicker than others, and some hit longer shots better than they do targets that are close. Most of us know our strengths, and we should take full advantage of them when we step into the station."

You need to decide where you want to shoot the target so that you'll be facing in the direction that will give you the most comfort, control, and body-to-gun fit at the time of the shot. "You'll basically want your body to face where you're going to break the target," instructs Murphy. "If you're a right-handed shooter, start off by simply pointing your left foot at where you're going to break the target. Your right foot will be pointed a little to the right."

Murphy uses the example of a clock, saying that if the target is to be broken at twelve o'clock, the right foot should basically be pointing somewhere around two o'clock. While it's important for the left foot to be pointing toward the point of the shot, the main thing is that the right foot be comfortable. "We all stand a little differently," he says. "The important consideration is that the right foot be placed naturally." (Again, I want to stress that this is for right-handed shooters. Southpaws will want to do just the opposite—point the right foot toward the point of the shot, and the left foot a little to the left.)

Hard crossing shots often require a little extra footwork. For the right-handed shooter, the fast left-to-right angles are the toughest because the swing of the gun goes against the body. If such a shot is going to be a real challenge, the shooter may actually want to point his front foot a little to the right for extra insurance and movement.

Most good shooters lean into the shot. Murphy estimates that about 60 percent of the shooter's weight is placed on the front foot.

Michael Murphy, a legendary gun fitter and sporting clays expert, shows how to set up for a shot. First he decides exactly where he wants to break the target.

Next he prepares for the shot. Once his gun is pointed where he wants to shoot, he'll twist his body so the barrel is about halfway back towards the thrower and he'll direct his eyes toward the point where he can first see the target. When the target is in sight it takes only a few smooth moves to make the shot.

Movement, he says, should be controlled by the back foot, with the gunner pivoting smoothly on the ball of that foot.

GUNHOLD

A shooter's height can have an effect on how he or she should hold the gun. Generally speaking, the shorter the shooter, the farther back toward the receiver the forward hand should be. Tall, long-armed shooters can reach farther out and still enjoy a smooth, continuous swing.

Sporting clays rules say that the gun can't be mounted until the target is in sight. Here Michael Murphy shows a good gun position while he waits. The gun butt is visible under the armpit and the muzzle is pointed at the target's line of flight.

Don't make the mistake of holding the gun too tightly. A viselike grip can cause jerky movements and increase your risk of flinching at the shot. Don't worry, the gun's not going to get away from you with a light hold.

Many shooters aid the natural shooting instinct by pointing with the index finger of the forward hand. Those who use semiautomatics and over/unders can point the index finger along the gun's stock or barrels. Side-by-side shooters can move the hand under the forearm so that the index finger is pointing between the two barrels. It's a little trick that some gunners really swear by.

In sporting clays, the gun must be held with the entire butt visible below the shooter's armpit. Like the forward hand, the back hand holds the grip firmly but lightly. In actuality, its main purpose is simply pulling the trigger.

Gun position, or more exactly, where the gun is pointing, can be of great importance. Far too many shooters make themselves endure too much gun movement. As with all aspects of shooting, the trick is to keep things as simple and fluid as possible.

Once in a good, proven stance, the shooter should slowly twist his upper body about halfway back toward where the target is first visible. The muzzle of the shotgun should be pointing in the same direction. This gun position will give the shooter time to get on the bird and develop a smooth swing before the actual shot, yet this swing will not be so long that the shooter will have trouble catching up with the target.

One very important ingredient is that the gun's muzzle should be in line with where the target will be flying. Those who keep the muzzle too low will lose precious time in raising the barrel, especially on a rapid target like a springing teal. A barrel that's too high or too low will also interfere with a smooth, effortless swing.

THE SHOT

Most experienced shooters and instructors recommend that the shooter turn only his eyes to where the target first appears. In most cases the target will quickly be seen after being called for, and from there will flow a chain of events that one hopes will be fluid and accurate.

Always take a few seconds to set up before calling for the bird. This shooter has picked a gap in the trees where he wants to take his shot and he's working on adjusting his stance and gun accordingly.

This shooter is exhibiting a good stance as he calls for the bird. When the target is in sight he'll smoothly mount his gun while turning his body. The odds are in his favor.

According to Murphy, the shooter's head should always be pointing out over the gun as his eyes track the target's flight. As the target passes the shooter, his body and gun begin to follow along. Again, the barrel should be pointed along the line of flight. The muzzle should show no more vertical movement than the increase or decrease of the target's flight.

The movement of mounting the gun is a lot like lifting a hinged lid. Imagine that the muzzle is vertically immobile and that the stock does all of the vertical movement. If you can do that, the muzzle will stay in line with the target, and the mount will take as little action as possible.

On some stations, such as a tower or long incoming shot, shooters will be able to see the target coming for several seconds before it's actually within range. Often the combination of anxiousness and anticipation will cause the shooter to shoulder the gun prematurely.

Try not to succumb to that temptation until just before it's time to take the shot. It's much easier to swing both the body and the gun when they aren't in contact with each other. The longer you keep the gun mounted in sporting clays, the greater the chance that you'll shoot behind the bird.

If all goes as planned and the gun fits the body well, both the eye and the muzzle will be looking at the exact same spot when the gun's butt is settled into the shoulder.

THE LEAD

Okay, let's say you have it down pat. Your stance is picture perfect as you look for the bird that you've just called. There! You see it coming and your body begins to pivot like a turret. Your gun's muzzle tracks the target as the butt of the shotgun slides smoothly into position. The gun and your body continue to swing as one as your finger tugs at the trigger. As the gun recoils, you see the target fly from sight—unbroken.

What happened? Obviously the target and the shot pattern missed meeting in the air. Your lead was wrong. Knowing that is the easy part; getting the right lead sometimes isn't so easy.

There are several schools of thought on how to ensure the proper lead for a flying target. Trap and skeet shooters often use a sustained lead. That is, they lead a certain target a set distance, and it will probably break. This technique, however, seldom works well in sporting clays. Unlike trap and skeet, in sporting clays there are no set angles and speeds. While you may be able to go to any skeet field in America and use the same leads on the same stations, it just doesn't work that way with sporting clays.

Many shooters use the "swing through and pull" method of shooting, and it's commonly taught to beginners by shooting instructors. It is very simple and for many very effective. Basically, the shooter calls for the bird and proceeds through the proper body movement, gun mount, and swing. While concentrating on the target, the shooter quickly swings the gun through the bird and pulls the trigger as he passes the front of the target, still continuing the swing.

Other shooters rely on a similar tactic that starts with the muzzle staying right on the target as the gun is being mounted. Once the gun is shouldered, the gunner keeps the muzzle on the target momentarily,

The running rabbit station is an excellent place to learn the "swing through and pull" method of shooting because it's about the only station where the target travels in a true straight line. A target on the ground also allows shooters to see exactly where they're shooting.

then pulls out in front "until it feels right" and pulls the trigger while continuing the smooth swing.

Still other sporting clays shooters bust their targets with no set game plan. For some, especially for avid shooters, hitting a flying target is purely instinctive. They're simply concentrating so hard on the target that they have no idea how far they're leading the bird.

What's the best technique? That will vary from shooter to shooter. What comes as second nature for one may feel unnatural to another. Shooting box after box of shells at sporting clays targets is the only way to find out what works best for you. Pick a pleasant, steady station where you can get the same shot time after time. Many courses will let you shoot as many targets as you want per station during practice.

Anytime you're working on shooting technique, try to do it in a quiet and relaxed atmosphere. Few shooters can devote their undivided attention to shooting when they're surrounded by a crowd of impatient shooters, all anxiously awaiting their turns at a station.

And don't rule out the possibility of using different shooting techniques on different stations. One of the joys of sporting clays is the variety of angles and speeds involved. Some gunners shoot instinctively at targets that are only in view for a few seconds but use the "pass and swing through and pull" technique on a long crossing shot that floats past for what seems like an eternity.

---5---

DOUBLE TROUBLE

As if I didn't have enough trouble breaking one target, many sporting clays courses give me twice the embarrassment, challenge, and fun by throwing two targets. The doubles of sporting clays add an extra element of realism and sport to target shooting. They're always enjoyable, especially once you've mastered how to break both targets.

Sporting clays basically uses three kinds of doubles. Simultaneous doubles are those that are thrown at the same time. A following target is a setup in which one target follows another within a short time. With on-report doubles, the second target is released when the trapper hears the first shot.

Sometimes a double is little more than two of the same basic targets being thrown. Under some circumstances, it can even be easier to hit the targets when two are thrown. If simultaneous targets are thrown from the same machine, the birds will be moving more slowly than a single. But this is a good-news/bad-news situation—although the targets will be slower, they'll also be going a shorter distance, which means you'll not only have to squeeze in two shots, but you'll also have to do it within a smaller area.

Concentration and a smooth gun swing are a must when shooting sporting clays. This shooter is about to pass through the right target, break it, and then move on to the next target.

Most instructors recommend turning the body slightly more toward the trap than usual. Such a move will often help the gunner get on the first target more quickly and allow for a faster swing on the second. According to the experts, minimizing gun movement and keeping things moving as smoothly as possible are keys to consistently breaking doubles.

A common combination will have a simultaneous pair of level or mildly climbing targets coming from the same trap. Many beginners will try to bust the front bird because it's the first in sight, and in theory, this saves time. Occasionally that *is* the best strategy, especially when the targets are in sight only momentarily. But usually the shooter will have more than enough time to pick up both targets. Smart shooters will wait and start with the back bird and then move to the front target in one continuous swing. It's usually much easier than breaking one target and backing up to find the next.

A lot of stations will use a pair of significantly different targets, for example, the popular fur and feather setup, which consists of a rabbit and a quartering or crossing bird. Pairs thrown on report require little special consideration. Simultaneous targets from different traps, on the other hand, take some thought.

Most good shooters like to spend a little time watching such a pair. A major part of the battle can be won simply by being familiar with the two targets. Study to see which target comes into sight first and which one vanishes last. Be aware that sometimes this can be the same target.

Let's take an example in which one target is a high crossing shot, such as from a tower, and the other target comes low to the ground, maybe even through brush. In the real world, it would be like pass shooting pheasants or ducks and having a quail or a woodcock flush at the same time.

Many shooters will want to start with the tower bird because they can usually see exactly where it's coming from. The problem with this is that by the time the shooter pulls the first shot, the second target may be falling and/or slipping from sight. It would probably be better to concentrate on the low bird first and take it when it gives the best opportunity—probably in an opening or at the peak of its short flight. Chances are good that you'll still be able to get a well-executed shot at the bird from the tower.

There are some other prime considerations as well. One is target size, which will determine how fast the target will fly and when it will start to drop. Usually the midis will be the fastest and farthest flying of the three popular target sizes. Minis, however, may be quick out of the gate, but their lack of weight causes them to lose velocity and head to the ground sooner. A falling mini is not exactly an easy target to break. Standard-size targets are in between the two in speed and are seen enough by most shooters to be pretty predictable.

If the flight time is equal, most experts prefer to try for the tougher of a simultaneous pair first so they can give it that extra bit of concentration. For instance, they'll try for the grouse target in the trees first and then move to a high overhead dove.

That concentration can be what separates the good doubles

shooter from the not so good. Too many shooters, myself included, make the mistake of rushing the first target in their haste to get to the second. A quick stab at the first target usually results in a missed bird and a poor swing to the second target.

It's important to really concentrate on the first bird and see it in your mind before you call for it. Never assume that you've broken it— watch to see that it breaks before you go on to the next target. Be sure

Larry Cero demonstrates how to work on a pair of targets. One is broken and he's already ahead of the other.

to keep the gun swinging after the first shot. If you've missed, it's usually best to go ahead and try the same target again. Chances are your miss was behind the bird. By the time you try again, you may be out in front where you should be.

The down side of trying the same target again is that you may have chipped the target but not seen the chip. Your odds are probably better sticking with target number one than switching to the second, because switching birds means more gun movement. An exception would be when the second target is a "gimme" like a slow floater or a shot that's your favorite. Again, some time spent studying the station first will help you make this kind of decision.

Another good consideration can be to take the low-flying bird first. For most of us it's much easier to bring the gun up to catch the next target rather than to drop it down. But here again there are always exceptions. Some courses offer "stations from hell," where the shooter faces a tall obstacle like a wall of trees and can't even glimpse the targets until they're falling in front of him.

Falling doubles are always tough, but it's a little simpler to start with the top bird. Since your swing will already be falling, it'll probably be easier to drop down and take the second bird—that is, if there's time.

Another thing to consider is which angle to take first, especially with targets that are crossing in opposite directions. Sure, it *feels* best to take the right to left first (assuming you're right-handed), but *is* that best? Possibly not. Many times it's wiser to take the harder left-to-right target first. That way, when you move to take the right-to-left target you'll be swinging with, rather than against, your body, and it will probably be faster and easier to catch up with the bird.

Every so often a gunner will get a chance to double up, or get two targets with one shot. Many courses will feature a simultaneous pair coming from opposite sides of the shooter. Often these targets will cross right in front of the station.

In such a case, breaking both with a single shot would be more luck than skill, and few instructors would encourage a shooter to plan on it. Many times such dreams of two with one do more harm than good, since the shooter will be tracking the bird he's not swinging on out of the corner of his eye. Such a distraction can lead to a variety of problems. It's better to concentrate on one target, smash it, and then let the second shot take care of the second bird.

Most times, the simpler you can keep a station the better. There are, however, times when a simultaneous pair thrown from the same trap will give a shooter a decent chance at busting both with one shot as the targets cross or pull within inches in midair.

Several years ago I was a judge at a station where a pair of midis came from a hilltop probably sixty to seventy yards from the left. Most shooters waited for the pair to get in front of the station, where they'd try for one bird at its peak and the other just as it began its fall.

One shooter decided to try something different. Noticing that the pair crossed about forty-five to fifty yards from the station, he screwed a full choke tube into one barrel while leaving the improved cylinder in the other. He stood in the far right corner of the wooden station, turned his body to face up the hill, and called for the first pair.

As had all the others, the targets came into sight and momentarily crossed in midair. The shooter began his mount when they came into sight, his cheek hitting the comb and his finger the trigger at just the right time, and both targets broke at the shot. At that range his pattern wasn't dense enough to do anything impressive, but I gave him a pair of Xs and watched.

He broke the next three pairs just as he had the first with a chip or two coming off of each target. But on the final pair just one of the targets broke. Keeping a cool head, the shooter dropped his gun back down and watched the second or two it took the target to move to directly in front of the station. When it did, he snapped his gun up and smashed the bird with his improved cylinder barrel. To say the least, he impressed everybody.

The next shooter tried to duplicate his feat but failed. As I recall, he only ended up with about a three of ten from the station. He simply didn't have the natural gift of making a quick shot on a long bird.

A few minutes later I was blessed with the opportunity to watch another shooter make the best of his natural ability. The gunner stepped into the box like all the others and called for the pair. The birds came into sight, crossed, then closed the distance and peaked twenty-five yards in front of the shooter. But he didn't fire. "It must be a malfunction," I thought. The shooter answered my question when he

This right-handed shooter is taking full advantage of the shooter's box to get as much room as possible on an angling double. His little trick will give him plenty of time to get on the second target.

busted the top target five feet below its peak. He broke the second target a mere five feet above the ground.

I watched in amazement as he ran ten for ten using the same strategy. "I've always been better at falling targets," he said with a shrug when I questioned his tactic. "Are there any more stations like this one? If there are I may be able to offset my poor showing on the rabbit and incoming prairie chicken."

Both of these shooters pulled perfect tens because they studied the station and considered their personal pluses and minuses.

SHOOTING
THE STATIONS

Though every sporting clays course is different, there are some common themes, which can call for similar shooting tactics. The following is an overview of these themes, including how some shooters successfully handle them.

No, simply reading these suggestions may not be enough to make an 80 percent shooter of someone who's struggling to break one out of four targets, but I hope this advice will get most shooters started in the right direction. If nothing else, it'll get you thinking about how you shoot the station. Sometimes such thinking is as important as natural ability.

SPRINGING TEAL

Last year I had the pleasure of leading a small group of outdoor writers through their first sporting clays shoot. We'd already shot the decoying duck, the woodcock target going through the trees, and left and right crossing stations that tried to duplicate flushing pheasant.

But it was station number five that raised the most eyebrows. With all looking on, I called, "Pull." A pair of targets launched nearly straight into the air from a pit twenty yards in front of the station. The targets rose like rockets, slowed momentarily, then seemingly fell as fast as they'd risen. "What do you think of springing teal?" I asked.

"It looks like a whole lot of fun," a friend answered. "That is, as long as someone else is shooting it. Why don't you show us how it's done?"

The fast climb of a pair of springing teal has had that intimidating

It is helpful to watch how others fare and learn from their successes and failures. This shooter, writer Bob Brister, is a great shot and has taught thousands how to improve their shotgunning over his long career.

effect on a lot of shooters. There are some, however, who say it's one of the easiest stations on a clays course. "I'd have to say that springing teal is now one of my favorite stations," says Sue King, a noted instructor and shooter. "I used to have some problems with it, then Bob Brister [of *Field & Stream* and *Houston Chronicle* fame] showed me how to do it."

"Like all sporting clays stations, it's important to know how to properly mount the gun. I'd recommend anyone who's having problems with that to go find a good instructor first. A lot of people haven't been exposed to how to do it properly."

King says that gun position is one of the keys to consistently breaking springing teal targets. Like all good shooters, King tries to study a station beforehand to familiarize herself with the shots. Once in the station, she'll go over the shot in her head while she gets into a good shooting stance. What happens next is of great importance.

"One of the biggest mistakes you can make is to have the gun pointing too low," King explains. "Some people really screw up by having the gun pointed just above the trap. That won't do; you won't be able to catch up with the targets in time to shoot them before they start falling. You need to start with a high gun hold. You want to be able to be right behind the bird and moving up with it as soon as you mount the gun. When you make your move up through the target, really sweep up through quickly and pull the trigger. You should break the target."

To some shooters, the fact that you can't see the target when you pull the trigger makes the vertical springing teal a problem. Concentration can be a big key to overcoming such a handicap. So can confidence. Break five in a row following King's suggestions, and you'll be shooting that way from then on.

The difference between springing teal singles and doubles, which are almost always simultaneous from the same trap, is a great one. A single springing teal can almost be a "gimme." Most gunners follow the bird until it slows near its peak and break it then. But if you do that on a pair, you'll be left trying to catch up with and hit a second target that's falling like a rock. Most good shooters try to take one target on the rise and one just before the peak.

King recommends that right-handed shooters start with the right

This hunter has just powdered a rabbit target as it bounded along the ground. Many shooters love the novelty of this station.

target first because it'll be easier and more natural to make the swing to the left target. Done properly, the shooter moves through the first target, breaks it, continues the vertical swing on up through the other target, and takes it in the same movement. It's often done so fast that the two shots seem tied together.

Naturally, not everyone has the reflexes to pull it off like that. But as King says, "A falling target is probably the most difficult. I make darn sure I try to take both of the springing teal targets *before* they start dropping."

RUNNING RABBIT

As with most shooters, it was love at first sight when I walked up to my first rabbit station. It's a shot that's so different from other target shooting that you can't help but like it—especially if you can hit the target.

As president and one of the founding members of USSCA, Bob Davis has certainly spent more than enough time at rabbit stations across America and in Europe. It's a station he claims to be one of his most consistent. Davis will spend some time observing and will have already decided where he wants to break the target before he steps into the station. His stance is so simple yet effective that it bears mention.

"Once I've made up my mind where I want to break the target, I'll set up so I'm facing right there," explains Davis. "I'll then turn my body maybe one-third to halfway back to where I can first see the target. Then I'll move just my eyes back to where I can get my first glimpse of the target."

Davis says that gunhold is of great importance. Most stations see the shooter with a rather high muzzle. According to Davis, that's a quick ticket to a miss on rabbit targets. "The biggest mistakes I see are having the gun too far back toward the trap [it takes too long to swing] and holding the gun above the rabbit's path. I like to try to keep the muzzle pointed just below where the rabbit will be crossing on the ground. That way I'm right on it and in no time I swing through it and break it. The guy who's got his gun too far back and pointed above the rabbit is going to need a lot more time, and there's a good chance he's going to shoot behind and/or above the target."

Fur and feather combinations require the shooter to do a little bit of preplanning and observation. It's usually easy to decide which to shoot first if both targets are thrown from the same spot. Most gunners take the rabbit quickly, then raise up and catch the bird as it's going in the same direction. A report pair isn't much different. A fur and feather in which the targets are at different angles can take a little more planning, but you can usually follow the basics of shooting doubles and do well.

One last consideration—rabbit targets are constructed a little harder than other targets in order to take the punishment of bouncing over rugged ground. For that reason, many gunners switch to a load with a little more power behind it, often opting for a course maximum of powder and 7½-size shot.

No matter how you shoot it, the rabbit station is one of the most fun things about sporting clays.

DECOYING DUCK
Properly set, the decoying duck station is one of the prettiest in sporting clays. There seems to be no end to the realism a designer can put

A shooter figuring out where to shoot the decoying duck station. This is one of the most popular stations in sporting clays.

into the stand. Quite often the shooter will step into an exact replica of a duck blind, complete with cattails, willows, and a placid pond. A few enterprising courses even send hunters out onto the water in a small boat. There are almost always mallard or pintail decoys scattered about for the icing on the cake.

It doesn't take a lot of imagination to convince yourself that it's the real thing—that is, until you call for the targets. Most times they'll come in high and from the side. Chances are you won't be able to see

He wisely tries to break both decoying duck targets before they begin their rapid fall towards the water. Here he broke the back target first and then swung on through the lead target and smashed it as well.

them until they're out in front of you. The targets, whether singles or doubles, will gently swing out and tilt themselves back into the decoys. But that's where the realism ends.

Most waterfowlers would let the ducks they're hunting land among the decoys and maybe watch them for several minutes before standing to take shots at the flushing birds. Sportsmen with less patience would stand when the birds were just above the decoys and try their luck at the ducks when they flare. Neither option works in sporting clays. Unless you break them, the targets are going to splash and dive deeper and longer than any scaup ever hoped to.

How you shoot the station depends a lot on the flight of the targets. If you're lucky, you may get a chance to pop the targets as they sail out over the water before they start down. If it's a single, the shot could be fairly simple. After watching a few birds, decide where you want to break the bird, get set up, and shoot it like a crossing shot.

Things can get complicated, however, if the target has been airborne for some time—then it could be falling at a slight angle. This can be a very deceptive shot. Watch out for this possibility when you're observing.

Just about any time you have a simultaneous double from the same trap, you're going to run into the problem of falling targets. Some shooters like to set up so they can take the first target almost the instant it comes into view, hoping that it won't be falling and they'll still have time to swing to the second bird before it plummets in among the decoys.

Sometimes the direction the targets are coming from will determine how you should set up. You need to set up differently for targets coming from left to right than for ones sailing in from right to left. Remember that it's best to set up so the gun swing will move into rather than away from a natural, comfortable shot. Mentally try both shots as you're setting up. Make sure you'll be able to get on the first target quickly and easily and still have room for a nice swing to the second duck.

Unfortunately, those dear souls who design these things usually make it so the shooter has little choice but to take at least one of the targets as it begins its fall. Shooting a target that's angling down rapidly isn't exactly an easy shot for many shooters. But as one designer says, "That's why they call it 'sporting' clays rather than 'easy' clays."

The trick is to get under the falling target and stay that way. If you have to, cheat a little going from target one to target two. Take the shortest route between two points and drop the muzzle in a line to the second target rather than following its circling flight path. Make sure you're well under it before you pull the trigger.

How far? That might vary a lot from gun to gun. A lot of guns have been designed to throw most of the pattern high to compensate for rising targets, and the higher the gun throws its pattern, the lower it'll have to be to bust a falling target.

There's also the little problem of the target's acceleration as gravity pulls it to earth. Chances are that if you miss, your shot will have been above the target. I've seen a lot of good shooters give themselves a second or two longer than on most other pairs to make sure they're under a falling second bird.

As with all difficult shots, there's no substitute for practice and a little gained confidence.

Driven Pheasant

A few years back I shared a goose-hunting blind with a pair of Michigan hunters. I listened to their tales of successes and tragedies on their Kansas "dream hunt" as we waited for daylight and the big Canadas it would bring.

"We probably had the most shooting at prairie chickens the last few days," said one. "I think we probably shot over a box apiece."

"That's a lot of shooting for prairie chickens," I commented.

"Yeah," said the second fellow, "especially for only three birds. The guide had us sitting so the birds were coming right at us, flying right over our heads, but it wasn't until it was almost time to leave that we started hitting them."

"Don't worry," I said. "Once you figure that shot out it'll be one of the easiest for the rest of your life."

A few minutes later a flock of a dozen geese came at us head-on, passing right over the blind. Two of us raised, fired once each, and watched as my golden retriever made one retrieve and then the other. "I know what you mean," said the hunter who'd fired. "I don't see how I ever missed all of those chickens. It was tough then but it's easy now."

The driven pheasant stations at most sporting clays courses are a lot like that. Modeled after high-flying pass shooting at the long-tailed birds in Europe, they usually feature targets that come high and from afar. Some courses will use a steep hill or ridge to get the targets above the gunner. Others will put the target throwers on a tower.

Sometimes the targets just suddenly appear above nearby trees, and other times you can watch them coming for what seems like an

This shooter is working on the popular driven pheasant station. It's a matter of covering up the target, continuing the swing, and pulling the trigger.

eternity. Either way, the basics for hitting the targets are essentially the same.

As always, try to spend a few minutes studying the situation before you decide on a game plan. Pay careful attention to where you can first see the target and its exact direction. Is it coming directly at you or slightly quartering at the last second? Is the bird basically flying in a straight line or is it losing altitude as it approaches?

Once you're in the station, try to set up where it will be the most comfortable to break the target. If you're shooting doubles, be sure to leave yourself plenty of room to smoothly swing to and through the second bird. Set up with the gun barrel just below where you want to break the target. If it's popping into view over a screen of trees and you want to break it quickly, you might want to point the gun at where the target will appear.

Most shooting instructors will tell you that one of the biggest mistakes made on a driven pheasant target is mounting the gun too early. It's sure tempting to shoulder the shotgun as soon as the bird's in sight, but to do so will slow you down so much that you'll never catch up with the target.

As mentioned earlier, a target flying head-on at you is one of the simplest to hit. (It must be—even I can do it!) It's basically a matter of mounting the gun with the muzzle just behind the birds, pulling up enough to block out the target, continuing the swing, and pulling the trigger. As long as you can't see the target when you're pulling the trigger you're in business.

With a pair of simultaneous doubles, you may need to rethink where you want to break the first target. The lead target, usually the second you'll shoot at, has a nasty habit of getting directly overhead before you know it. Such a shot is often made impossible by the safety bar at the top of the station. Even when you *can* give it a try, it can be difficult to bend your body back far enough to get a smooth swing with your face still on the gun's stock.

When possible, it's often best to try to break the first bird—the back of the pair—a little sooner than you would if it were a single. That should give you plenty of room to try a crack at the other target while it's still at a reasonable angle.

The first time I shot such a station I switched my Ruger's selector to the modified barrel and broke the first target when it was probably thirty to thirty-five yards out. I caught up with the other target about seventy degrees up and smashed it as well. It was one of the few good ideas I actually had on my own that day. I shot the station twice and had no problem running twenty straight. Those who know me will tell you just how rare that is!

Wood Pigeon or Darting Dove

The wood pigeon station is fashioned after a popular sport in Europe in which hunters try to bring down fast-moving targets that appear and disappear quickly among the treetops. The closest thing I can find to it in America is probably standing in the middle of a good dove roost and trying to connect with the feathered missiles as they zip about through and above the trees. Unlike a grouse or woodcock station, it's usually modeled after pass shooting, rather than flushing, birds.

It presents the shooter with a pair of problems: His view of the bird is partially obstructed by tree trunks, leaves, and branches, and he is trying to hit what is often a quick target that's only in sight for a few moments. It's not uncommon for a course to use minis or midis to add further realism (and humility to the shooter).

The first step, as you no doubt have already guessed, is to spend some time studying the situation. Pay careful attention to exactly where the targets come into view. Don't settle for "somewhere over there"; try to figure out exactly which branch they're going to appear over first.

Concentrate on the birds' flight paths as they sail past and watch for the best opening among the trees for a shot. This may be where the birds first pop into sight or where they're just about to go out of sight. On most stations, however, there will be a few openings to choose from.

Try to have a firm game plan in mind when you set up in the station, and stick to it. Don't let the presence of the trees and leaves pysch you out. Ignore them as best you can.

A good shooter usually points the muzzle at the edge of the clearing where he wants to break the bird so he'll be able to react as quickly as possible when the bird comes into the open. Concentrate heavily on the bird once you've called for it. Keep your eyes on the exact place you've determined it will appear and don't take them off the bird after it comes into sight. Follow the bird with your eyes its entire trip. Even when you can't see it behind a group of trees, keep your eyes moving along the same line and at the same speed. You'll want to be ready when it pops back into view.

Knowing your abilities can be of great importance on such a station. Good snap shooters, those who seem to be able to break a target

Many courses feature targets going through the woods. It adds to both the realism and the challenge.

the instant they see it, can have a big advantage. Some quick-acting gunners will pick an opening and simply focus their eyes on it, not wanting to get confused or overanxious by watching the target fly in and out of sight as it approaches.

Don't be afraid to shoot through a little brush or when the target goes behind a small tree. Your shotgun pattern is wide, and not all pellets arrive at the same time. Generally speaking, if you can get even a glimpse of the target, a well-made shot will find a way of breaking it.

Doubles through the treetops can be interesting, to say the least. Sometimes they'll offer an opening large enough for the shooter to break both targets with a quick "boom-boom," as with springing teal. Occasionally you'll have to wait for the second target to pass behind some timber before you get a chance at it. Don't make the mistake of slowing your swing just because you can't see the target or are only getting a partial glimpse of it—try to stay even with your target so you can make your move and shatter it when you get your chance.

Every once in a while you'll come across a station where you have to swing on an almost invisible target for quite some time. I once had a pair come into view twenty yards to my right but remain all but hidden by the treetops until they were twenty yards to my left. A lot of shooters were breaking a bird in each opening. How'd I do? As my dad occasionally used to say, "Do as I say, not as I do."

POTPOURRI

There are several common sporting clays shots that are not known by standard names but are often named after local gamebirds that present similar challenges. Even though the names may vary, the concepts and strategies are still very similar from course to course.

High Going Away

This situation is modeled after one of the most frustrating shots in wing shooting. There you sit, watching for the ducks you know are going to come from the south, and then they do it—they come straight out of the north. Sometimes they're almost out of range before you can see them and react.

It's a little easier than that in sporting clays because, having watched the station, you know the target's flight plan and you know it'll come into view within seconds after you mutter the magical, bird-producing word "pull." But no matter what, the target almost always seems to just suddenly appear, moving faster than you'd really like. For some, it's one of the most challenging stations on the course; for others, the shot is nearly as automatic as with the cover-the-bird-and-break-it-every-time high incoming driven pheasant station.

There are a few subtle tricks of the trade for consistently breaking such a target. Again, one of the keys is keeping things as simple as possible. Since it's difficult to see the target approach, because it's coming from behind, some shooters go to inappropriate lengths to prepare for the shot. I've seen shooters lean so far back you'd have sworn they were doing the limbo. Their shots wound up being far from smooth as the shooters worked to keep their balance and catch up with the fast-flying targets.

Another case of severe overcompensation involved a fellow who set up facing straight ahead, pointed his gun muzzle in the right direction, then twisted his whole body as far as possible to the left. The fast movement of his body made it all but impossible to get a proper, consistent gun mount.

Most good shooters go through the regular basics of setting up for where they plan to break the targets. But one important thing that separates them from those who have trouble with the station is what they do with their bodies: not a heck of a lot. A good shooter simply tilts his head back a little, rolls his eyes up to look for the bird, then calls for it. If all goes as planned, the bird will come into sight, and his eyes will follow it as his head drops straight down to meet the gun as it's being mounted. If the gun fits properly, the muzzle will be pointing where the shooter is looking, which should be right at the target.

One important thing to remember when setting up for such a shot is that the gun barrel should not block your view. In other words, don't have the gun too high. Normally, it should be about halfway between where you first see the target and where you hope to shoot it.

Sometimes it'll be necessary to hold the gun slightly to one side or the other so the barrel(s) won't block the flight of the bird. We're not talking about anything drastic—just an inch or so to the side so you can watch the bird. Generally, right-handed shooters move the gun a shade to the right, and left-handed gunners to the left. Don't overdo it; you still want to be able to have a smooth and consistent gun mount.

Okay, so you've got the target in sight, the gun mounted, and your eyes looking right down the barrel. Now comes the tricky part: actually hitting the target. The high going away can be a deceiving station; though it appears to be a basic straightaway, it actually requires the basic principles of shooting a falling target. One key is to let the gun fall smoothly through the target. It may feel a little unnatural, but it's an absolute must for consistently breaking the targets.

If you opt for pass-through shooting, track the target, drop the muzzle through it, and pull the trigger as soon as you can see daylight between the muzzle and the target. Still, the importance of allowing the barrel to continue to fall can't be stressed enough.

Quartering, Coming In

A shot that's generally not too complicated, a quartering target coming at the shooter lends itself well to the traditional set-up-and-swing-through style of shooting. Be sure to have the barrel pointed along the target's line of flight. Don't rush the gun mount if you have to wait for the target. As always, the longer you have to swing the gun, the more likely you are to end up behind the target.

Don't make the mistake of overriding the target. If you use the swing-through tactic, hit the trigger as soon as you see daylight between the barrel and the bird as it passes. If you shoot instinctively, take your shot the instant things feel right. One possible problem: the target may rise or fall as it quarters at you. If the target has been airborne long, it'll probably be feeling the effects of gravity as it nears. Pay attention as other shooters try their luck. If the bird is falling, you'll have to figure out how to get both in front of and below the target.

Quartering, Going Away

A quartering shot going away is common in the worlds of both hunting and sporting clays. It's often fairly easy; however, a lot of courses spice it up with something to make it a little tougher, such as trees.

You should usually set up in the standard position regardless, with your body facing where you want to break the bird, your gun and your head about halfway back to the target, and your eyes directed toward

What often looks like an easy shot can sometimes be deceptive. Though these targets appear to cross straight across, they're actually slowing and losing altitude.

where you'll first see the target. Don't make the mistake of rushing your mount and swing. Problems can arise if you let the barrel get ahead of the target before it's time to shoot. You'll want to be accelerating going into the shot. Most who start out ahead of the bird will find themselves slowing or pausing for the shot, either of which will usually result in a miss. As with any crossing shot, you'll need to decide whether the target is on the level, rising, or dropping and adjust accordingly.

Again, every station on every course is different. But if you can master a few basic shots, you should be able to adjust them to just about anything a course designer can throw.

WOMEN'S CLAYS

Had you happened to drive past Houston's American Shooting Center that blustery May morning, you surely would have noticed all the activity at the sporting clays course. Granted, clays tournaments are seemingly as common as oil fields in the state that first hosted this American craze, but those who looked closely enough could easily tell there was something very special about this particular shoot.

One thing was its size. A steady stream of cars moved along the meandering road past the rifle, pistol, trap, and skeet ranges and finally emptied into a huge mass of parked autos that engulfed both the regular lot and surrounding fields. Those who know the sport would instantly realize they were witnessing one of the largest shoots in the country.

Approximately 240 shooters followed a circular path that led them past such usual gunning stations as spring teal, high flying dove, and fast crossing grouse. The grounds were filled with what seemed to be at least an equal number of spectators, who added shouts of encouragement, good-natured laughter, and an occasional round of applause to the steady chatter of gunfire.

As is becoming increasingly common, there were a lot of families touring the course. But unlike many tournaments in the past, the men were pushing the strollers and the women were carrying the Brownings and Berettas. In fact *every* one of the shooters was a woman. It was the third annual Ladies Charity Classic.

One of the event's most important functions was to raise over $17,000 for a local battered women's and children's shelter. Another was to help showcase the growing number of women who are interested in the shooting sports—a good number of whom are entering via sporting clays.

Frankly, it's about time!

Since the day of the matchlock musket, societies have looked at shooting as a sport (and business) of men. Hopefully those days are finally in the past.

"It's still a commonly held belief that shooting isn't for women, and that's been keeping a lot of interested women away," says Sue King, a vivacious organizer of the shoot and a nationally respected sporting clays instructor. But women seem to be realizing that it's not for males only. In fact, it's one of the few sports in which men don't have a predetermined advantage.

"Shooting is the perfect sport for women," remarks King, whose clays scores are the envy of even the best male shooters. "You don't have to be stronger or quicker or have exceptionally great reflexes to do well at sporting clays. All you have to do is swing a shotgun, stand in one spot, and say 'pull.' It's the easiest sport in the world to learn. It's much easier than bowling, tennis, or golf."

The main ingredient is a little hand-eye coordination. That's something many women have plenty of, especially those who enjoy such sports as volleyball, softball, and running. Some are simply naturals for shooting sporting clays.

Shellie Collier of Dallas was a prime example. A retail marketing representative for Olin-Winchester, the young and athletic Collier had never fired a round at sporting clays. In fact, her entire shooting career up to this event included just a pair of shoots at a skeet range.

With her permission, I followed Collier from station to station at the Ladies Charity Classic. My goal was to write about how even beginners can have a great time even if they break only a few targets. Well, Collier did have a great time, but she broke more than a few.

Shellie Collier of Dallas has good reason to be happy: she just broke thirty-four of fifty targets on her very first shoot! She's excellent proof that sporting clays is a sport for both men and women.

After going just one for four on each of the first two stations Collier got on a roll. With the helpful advice of a coworker, the triathlete was able to bust the next eleven targets and ended the round of fifty with an impressive 34!

"I thought it was a lot of fun," Collier said after her final station. "All I had to do was watch the angles and speed and then let my instincts take over."

Nevertheless, as is the case with men, a good percentage of beginning women shooters need a little assistance. No doubt thousands of women have been introduced to clay target shooting with an inexpensive target thrower.

Once the basics such as proper gun mount have been mastered, a few simple, eye-level, straightaway targets can be thrown. Once a few are broken, the person is usually hooked. But experts like King think it best if a woman's husband or father *doesn't* do the hooking.

"In my experience a husband should never attempt to teach his wife to shoot," advises King. "In fact, I won't even let a husband watch if I'm giving a woman a lesson, and if I'm giving a man a lesson I don't want his wife around either. The shooters are always aware that someone else is watching them, and they'll often try too hard. I'd rather have them relaxed so they can do exactly what we say."

Whenever possible, King recommends that a woman take her first lessons from an experienced woman shooter. "One of the big draws of the Ladies Classic is that we offer free lessons, taught entirely by women, the weekend before the shoot. I'm convinced having women instructors is what gets a lot of the real beginners out here. We have quite a few who show up not knowing if they're shooting a shotgun or a rifle. But we can have them breaking at least a few targets when they leave . . . that's all it takes and they're hooked."

According to King, the equipment is often more of a problem than natural ability. Too many men, she says, are putting their own rejects in the hands of a woman. "You'd be amazed at some of the crap women show up with. For some reason a lot of men send their wives or whoever out here with exactly the wrong kind of gun. There are two extremes: Either they come with a super-lightweight gun that kicks them silly, or they show up with something that's so big and heavy they can't do anything with it. You'd also be surprised at how many full chokes show up."

Because of their generally smaller bodies, King recommends that women stay away from the heavyweight gauges and loads. "A lot of men like to have their wives shoot a real heavy load," King comments. "I think they should shoot the lightest load they can get for their gun. There's no reason for a social shooter to take the punishment of an ounce-and-a-quarter or an ounce-and-a-eighth load. One ounce of shot can break every target on the course and it doesn't kick much. It's impossible for someone to really have a good time if she takes a beating at every station."

When it comes to gun fit, a lot of people worry about the stock length for a woman, but just because a shooter is a woman doesn't mean you automatically need to saw off a stock. Of all gun measurements, cast is probably the most important because a woman's shoulders are obviously built differently than a man's because of their chests.

Women who get the right equipment and practice religiously can achieve some remarkable clays scores. Pris McClaugherty won the Ladies Charity Classic with an impressive score of 45; three other women had scores above 40.

Though scores were kept, competition was but a minor part of the shoot. A good percentage of the scores were in the teens, usually turned in by beginning shooters. According to King and other organizers, that was the group they were trying to recruit.

"I got a 17 and I really didn't expect to do that well," said Pam Griffin of Houston. "I just got my first gun in September. I'm already planning to come out next week, and I'm going to help with the shoot next year . . . it's in my blood."

Similar words were spoken by every woman I talked with; those who were shooting for the first time promised that it wouldn't be their last. I witnessed a lot of new friendships being made, and women who didn't know each other until the morning of the shoot were already setting up groups to shoot every week or month.

Those who take up the sport often stand to gain more than their own enjoyment. "Many women who shoot here are professional women," King pointed out. "They're discovering that it really helps them in business if they're able to shoot. Here in Texas so many of our corporations have bird leases." All across the nation, corporate America is spending more and more time entertaining on sporting clays courses.

Even more important is the personal appeal of the sport. In these days when families spend less and less time together, sporting clays can be a common bond that all members, regardless of gender, can enjoy.

"I got really interested in shooting when I went to my son's hunter safety courses with him," says Griffin. "I could see what he and his father were going to be doing and I didn't want to be left at home. I really, really enjoy it."

There is another very important reason why avid shooters should

Sue King is one of the true founders of American sporting clays. Like many shooters, King obviously favors an over-under with fairly long barrels for a smooth, steady swing.

be striving to get more women involved in the sport. As you surely know, guns and shooting are under increasingly heavy attack. When the war is won it won't be by those of us who already cherish guns or those who currently want them abolished. No, the deciding votes are yet uncast—many of them by women.

"We definitely need to get more nonshooters involved, especially the women," said F. Carter "Sandy" Wood, Shooting Promotions Manager, Winchester. "They're a major, major voice in this country. We think they're extremely important."

In some ways, the women's presence at a sporting clays shoot is just as important as their personal opinion. "The average person equates a gun with a man and violence," says King. "If they can see or hear about 240 women having a blast with shotguns, it's going to tone down much of the hysteria about guns and violence."

Wood agrees: "Women who shoot lend credence to the fact that the shooting sports are okay. The more of them who give their blessings to shooting, the more we quell some of the negativism that we're now fighting."

If the grounds of the Ladies Charity Classic are any indication, it would appear that the sporting goods companies are more than willing to do their share to get more women involved in shooting.

Mike Hampton of the NSCA worked long hours to set up and furnish the traps for the shoot. Wood said that Winchester gladly donated all of the ammo that was shot during the competition. White Flyer was quick to furnish the cases of clay targets that were used. Browning donated a half dozen shotguns. Other companies donated dozens of prizes ranging from expensive hunting clothing to free guided hunts. Each entrant was also awarded a "goody bag" filled with enough merchandise to all but equal out their $50 entry fee.

As has been the case from year to year, the fourth annual Ladies Charity Classic in 1991 will no doubt draw many more women shooters than did the third. And "Ladies' Nights" (evenings when women can shoot for half price) are becoming increasingly popular at sporting clays ranges across the nation.

The table appears to be set—now we just need to get more men to take their wives, girlfriends, mothers, daughters, and sisters for a pleasant day at a sporting clays course. All it usually takes is a little laughter in the fresh air and a few broken targets to ignite the fire that will let the future of shooting in America grow just a little brighter.

MIND GAMES

Kansas's Tim Murphy summed it up best as he drove to the final day of the 1990 USSCA Championship in Colorado Springs. "A lot of it's a mind game," said Murphy, who arrived as an unknown and left with a medal and the respect of the world's best shooters. "Once you can physically break all of the targets, all you have to do is do it. A lot of that's in your mind."

Dr. Michael Keyes, a prominent psychiatrist and avid sporting clays shooter and author, agrees. "In all clay target shooting the targets aren't really that hard to hit. We possess the physical ability to operate the gun well enough to break the target," says Keyes. "Much of it is having the right mind-set. It's a different mind-set than with trap or skeet."

Unlike trap and skeet, sporting clays isn't a sport of simple repetition. Every station and course is different. According to Keyes, that's an important consideration.

"It's best to think of sporting clays as a series of one-shot matches," Keyes advises. "You have to prepare for and handle every target one at a time. As soon as you shoot at one target you start all over getting ready for the next."

Frustration and a lack of confidence can be real enemies on the clays course. Try to stay calm and figure out why you may be having trouble with a shot.

As with any game that involves fluid mind, eye, and hand coordination, relaxation is a major piece of the puzzle. There's no way a shooter who is a bundle of frayed nerves can pull it all together well enough to shoot a good round of clays.

"Proper planning can be very important for staying relaxed," Dr. Keyes emphasizes. "You should make sure you're prepared for anything before you step out onto the course. The less you have to worry about, the better."

Keyes, who has coached many shooters through a regular column in *Shotgun Sports* magazine and as a doctor for the 1980–1984 U.S. Olympic Shooting Team, recommends developing a regular routine for getting relaxed. One method is to stand, sit, or lie still, taking deep, regular breaths. Clench your fists tightly for ten or fifteen seconds, then abruptly relax your grip. You should feel the tension flow out of your fingertips. Repeat this several times, then work your way through your whole body, tensing and relaxing each area's muscles: arms, shoulders, feet, legs, stomach, chest, neck, and face.

Using this systematic technique, a shooter can achieve total relaxation. Keep in mind that it can take a great deal of practice to master, but once learned it is a valuable tool that can be used anywhere, anytime.

Being able to break the target in your mind can also be an important step towards success. "The idea is to figure out and visualize beforehand what you're going to do once you step up . . . and then do it," says Keyes. "Don't listen to anyone else, unless he's your coach. You know what you can do best, so plan for it."

Most shooters who are at their mental best will visualize the entire scene before they call for the target. They'll mentally see the target coming through the air, they'll mentally feel the gun come up, the barrel swing, and the shot fire, then see the target breaking.

"Try to visualize the mental rehearsal in as much detail as possible," says Dr. Keyes. "It primes your body, and you should be able to make the shot smoothly and naturally. Once you actually take the shot, you go through the entire process again. Clear your mind, relax, visualize the shot, and do it again."

The whole routine can be especially important if an unsettling situation should arise—like a "no bird" or an unusual miss. "If you have a problem, it's important to totally back off, clear everything from your mind and relax," Keyes recommends.

One of the biggest mental friends or enemies of sporting clays is simple confidence. If you don't think you can break a target, you probably won't. Those who have never had confidence may want to invest in a good coach to help them consistently break targets. Those who have lost their confidence needn't worry. They can get it back with a little mental work. "Don't consider it anything lost," says Keyes. "See it as a new challenge that can be overcome."

If you've done it before, you can do it again. Sometimes it's best to back up to the strengths that you know you have. If you can still shoot one station well, go back and do it over and over again until you are relaxed and confident. Then go to the problem station. If you're still having problems, get a good coach. He may put you on the right track in a matter of minutes.

Like all aspects of shooting sporting clays, the mental side of the game is something that can't be forgotten. It's not a lot of work, but it can pay huge dividends. "Just as you train physically to be a good shooter, you have to train mentally," says Dr. Keyes.

Talk to any successful shooter or coach and they'll agree with him 100 percent.

LESSONS

I was a prime candidate for shooting lessons. In the field I usually shoot well at worst, and I also hold my own at the trap park. But my sporting clays average wasn't up to par with that of my wing shooting or trap shooting. To make matters worse, my scores were falling rather than improving. My confidence was at an all-time low.

No doubt about it, I needed professional help. I was a prime candidate for shooting lessons. So are:

- Shooters who consistently shoot a low score. For an experienced shooter, that would be shooting less than 50 percent on the sporting clays field.

- New shooters who have little to no experience with shotguns. Actually, these students are an instructor's dream—no experience means no learned bad habits. Such a student is "like a piece of unshaped clay," one instructor says. "You can mold it any way you want. It's easier to start from scratch and do it right the first time."

- Gunners who are shooting inconsistently—very high one day and very low the next or running one station but busting just one of ten on another.

Shooting lessons can be geared toward the very basics or teach the intricate details, such as how to break a pair of battues screaming through the trees.

It's easy to get help. The problem is getting the proper help. Every time my frustration would show at a station, I'd be bombarded with well-meaning advice: "You're shooting low," "I think you were about four feet behind the target," "You're checking your swing," and "Aim for the front of the target and you'll get it, you're that close." And all of that coaching on a single station!

A number of good shooters offered to take me under their wings and try to show me the ropes as they pulled them. But I knew that the wrong kind of coaching would only complicate the problem. So I turned to a proven, professional shooting instructor—my good friend and USSCA-certified coach Michael Murphy.

Murphy is far from the only good coach in the nation, but a potential student can't latch on to just anyone and expect him to iron out his problems. The USSCA has a list of veteran instructors for the asking. No doubt the NSCA could also recommend a potential teacher. Many established sporting clays courses also have professional instructors based at their facilities.

It never hurts to shop around before you decide on an instructor. If possible, try to shoot a round with the pro. See if he or she uses a style you'd be comfortable with. Obviously, you'll want to see how well the person shoots—it would make no sense to listen to someone who shoots worse than you do.

And don't be afraid to switch instructors once you've had a lesson or two. If you aren't comfortable with an instructor, you probably won't get your money's worth. This doesn't mean you should have every lesson from a different teacher. Just make sure you have a coach who's enjoyable and able to show you improvement.

Having spent hundreds of hours talking clays with Murphy, I was confident he could get me pointed in the right direction. Like a lot of

Beginners are far better off going straight to an experienced instructor. This learner will be amazed at how quickly she'll start breaking targets once she gets off on the right foot.

shooters, I swallowed my ego, admitted I needed help, and called to set up a lesson.

For the purpose of this book I had him start at the beginning. The first step was to make sure my gun fit. According to Murphy, a recognized expert on the subject, sometimes outfitting the shooter with a shotgun that fits the body is half the battle. Having measured me in the past, Murphy knew my battered Ruger Red Label fit me fine. A little checking showed that my new Browning GTI would cause me to consistently shoot high. Though the Ruger's short, twenty-six-inch barrel and fixed chokes make it less desirable than the Browning, it would have to do until I could get the Browning's stock bent. The other alternative would be to get another gun.

The next step was to work on gun mount. "There's no way that could be a problem," I thought. "I hit quail and doves too well." Murphy wasn't so sure. "I haven't given a lesson to a problem shooter yet where they didn't have at least a small problem with their mount," he said. "That includes some great target [trap and skeet] shooters. In their sport they get to make sure the mount is right before they call for the target. It's not that way in sporting clays."

We checked my mount with an unloaded gun, then headed to a trap. "We want to get started with targets that require as little swing as possible," said Murphy. "We usually start out right beside the trap to keep it simple. He watched as I called for, shot at, and missed or barely nicked some targets that climbed from right to left.

He soon ruled out a fairly common problem. "A lot of people simply can't see the target very well for a wide variety of reasons," Murphy explained. "Sometimes they don't see it in time to have a

A little advice from a qualified coach can go a long way. Here the author turns to Gordon Philip for tips on how to up his percentages on long crossing shots.

chance at breaking it. Any time they're having problems seeing the target I recommend they go to an eye doctor. I've had several people who didn't realize they needed glasses until they got on the sporting clays course."

After a few targets, the instructor began picking up a few inconsistencies in my stance. We reviewed how to set up properly, with the body facing where we want to break the target and the feet in the proper stance to allow smooth body movement.

I went through a few setups, and Murphy spotted a problem. I was starting out fine but running into a problem when I pivoted halfway back to the trap. Unknown to me, I was dipping my body slightly toward the trap. The result was a complicated gun mount and swing. "Your lower body should be doing the moving," coached Murphy. "You want your upper body to stay as immobile as possible." He showed me what I was doing wrong and then how to do it properly. He was right. No matter if it's the golf swing of Arnold Palmer or the bat action of George Brett, the trick is to make things smooth, consistent, and simple.

Murphy offered a little quick advice on gunhold and stock position while we were waiting for the target. Like a proper pivot, this problem was also easily corrected once I was aware of it.

My next fault, however, wouldn't be so quickly corrected. "This time, pay careful attention to your gun mount," Murphy directed. "Look what you're doing with your head." I set up, turned my eyes back toward the trap, and called for the bird. I pivoted my body to follow its path, raised the gun, and fired shortly after the stock hit my cheek. "Stop," Murphy instructed. "Look how you have the gun mounted."

As he had observed, I was short-stopping the gun on the way to a proper mount. In fact I was even dropping my head to meet the stock. There was no way I could shoot or swing consistently while doing this.

I backed away from where I had been standing and went through some practice mounts, first in slow motion and then at a regular speed. Murphy took the gun and showed me what I was doing wrong. It seemed inconceivable for someone who shoots birds as well as I to have such a basic problem. It's embarrassing to have shot for twenty years and find out you need to go back to kindergarten for sporting clays.

I stepped back up, loaded the Ruger, set up, and called for a bird.

A young woman gets some coaching from an experienced shooter. By looking right over her shoulder he can offer valuable advice on how to improve her technique.

After the missed shot, I noticed I'd improperly mounted the gun again. Murphy and I talked about the problem. I had a nice mount in practice and no doubt in bird shooting as well, but it was still poor in sporting clays, even once I was aware of it. Why?

I can only guess. I think it's been a fairly recent occurrence, something I didn't do when I first started the sport. It's quite possible that my early problems caused me to try to rush my mount. My frustration over missing targets was making things worse instead of better.

"You can rush the shot but never, never rush the mount," said Murphy. "It needs to be smooth and consistent." He took the gun, set up, and called for a bird. He talked his way through a mount that seemed to be in slow motion. Even so, he powdered the target in plenty of time. "Watch only the mount," he said as he busted five or six straight targets.

I stepped up, called for the bird, and leisurely brought the gun up. The target broke at the shot, as did the next and the next. I relaxed, took a small break, and then confidently stepped up to take another shot. The next two targets flew off unscathed by the shot. But I wasn't surprised. I could tell when I pulled the trigger that my mount had been rushed and poor. There was, however, a little joy even in the misses. Thanks to Murphy I was now conscious of my errors. That in itself was half the battle.

Murphy suggested that I practice my mount while looking in a mirror at home. "You want to concentrate on making it smooth and consistent," he instructed. "In your case, try to visualize yourself actually shooting a station. You'll also need to work on concentrating on your mount whenever you shoot sporting clays."

Normally he would have stopped the lesson there. "You don't want to overload a student with too much," he explained. "Some lessons only last twenty minutes. We generally only take on one problem at a time. Sometimes it takes two or three lessons just to overcome one fault."

After a break we moved on to another problem—my consistently shooting behind the targets. My coach watched over my shoulder as I tried crossing shots. Those I hit were chipped at the back of the target. Others were cleanly missed behind.

"Try to visualize a long neck on the target and shoot it in the head," Murphy suggested. It's a trick that's worked for many of his students, but it didn't work for me. Time after time Murphy called my shots: "You're getting ahead of the bird, and you either totally stop your swing or slow it down when you pull the trigger."

My problem was that, despite all of my shooting, I'd never mastered the swing-through method. For close shots on birds, I learned, I was using snap shots. On long shots I was using a sustained lead.

Murphy sent me home to practice a swing that would be consistently smooth even after the shot. The line where the wall meets the ceiling would serve as the flight path of an imaginary target. A snap-cap in the gun's barrels would provide me with as much realism as possible.

When I return for my next lesson, we'll pick up where we left off. "I rarely have someone take just one lesson," said Murphy. "There's no magical thing an instructor can do to suddenly turn someone into an excellent shot. It takes time—and shells." Luckily, I have the time and he has the ability to help me make the most of it.

No, lessons don't come for free. In 1990 Murphy was charging $50 an hour plus targets. That's a fair amount, but not that much more than a mechanic charges to work on your car, or a plumber to work on your pipes. Most gunners value their shooting ability as much as either. Look at it as an investment. The better you shoot, the more you enjoy shooting. If you've already sunk hundreds, probably thousands, of dollars into guns, accessories, shells, and course fees, the cost of a few lessons seems relatively low.

10

GUNS

Without a doubt the most important and fascinating piece of sporting clays equipment is the shotgun. Though it sometimes seems as though I could do better throwing rocks, there's no arguing the advantages of having the best gun possible.

What makes a good sporting clays shotgun? A lot is up to the shooter. If you're more dedicated to bird hunting than to target shooting and you're facing a limited budget, your best sporting clays gun will probably be your trusty old bird gun. There's a lot to be said for using the same gun you carry in the uplands or marshes. Sporting clays is a phenomenal way to sharpen your wing-shooting skills. Spend a day or two a month busting rocketing clay targets and you'll be more than ready for opening weekend. Some shooters report that since they took up sporting clays their average on wild birds has doubled, with far fewer cripples.

GAUGE

Those who are truly serious about sporting clays will tell you that it's a 12-gauge game. When you're up against shooters who are using the ultimate in power and pellet count, it's tough to compete with anything less.

It's worth mentioning that a few tournaments are featuring special classes for small-gauge shooters. Though not usually as lethal as a 12 gauge, 16, 20, and 28 gauges have turned in some very impressive scores. Real deadeyes can bust their share of targets with the comparatively little .410 as well.

Basically, if you shoot for fun, shoot whatever you want to; but if you're in competition, whether against yourself, your buddies, or the best that America and Europe have to offer, go with the old reliable 12 gauge.

ACTION

Go to just about any local, regional, or national tournament, and you'll quickly see that the over-under shotgun is the heart and soul of sporting clays. While judging a station at a national shoot, I tallied the over-unders, and they outnumbered other gun actions by about ten to one.

There are many advantages to having a pair of stacked barrels. One is ease in pointing and swinging. A balanced over-under that fits the shooter will point as easily as if it were an extension of the person's eye. The even distribution of the barrels' weight from breech to muzzle helps the gun swing smoothly.

A pair of barrels also gives the shooter some added flexibility when he steps into a station. There are times when having two different chokes in a gun can be a real advantage, for example, when you're shooting a fur-and-feather station that starts with a fifteen-yard crossing shot at a rabbit with a simultaneous midi quartering away. If you were shooting a single-barrel gun, you'd probably split the difference and shoot an improved cylinder. But with two barrels, you could try the rabbit with a skeet choke and then take your time and bust the other target with a modified.

A side-by-side shotgun would give a shooter the same flexibility, yet you'll see very few of them on a sporting clays course. One reason could be expense. You can usually get a lot more shotgun for your money with an over-under than with a side-by-side of equal value.

This shooter is using a quality over-under for his clays shooting. Almost any gun will work for sporting clays. The important thing is that the shooter have a good and safe time.

Some shooters also claim to be distracted by the wide sight plane of a side-by-side. Also, over-unders seem to be growing in popularity among wing shooters.

One last interesting point regarding the over-under versus side-by-side debate is that although the side-by-side is the gun of tradition and choice for British hunting, most sporting clays shooters will carry an over-under to the course. Remember, these are the people who've been doing it for generations.

Call them what you want—autoloaders, automatics, or semiautomatics—single-barrel guns that fire and put another shell in the chamber at the pull of the trigger are probably the second most popular action for sporting clays.

No doubt a lot of clays shooters have hunted with automatics for years, and it seemed only natural to take this type of gun to the sporting course. Automatics have less felt recoil than fixed breech guns. Cost can also be a factor. Some of the finest automatic shotguns in the world can be bought for a few hundred dollars less than a bottom-line over-under.

But it's worth mentioning that some shooters who could have whatever they want are spending more and more time with automatics in their hands. The 1990 USSCA National Championships in Colorado Springs are a perfect example. Two of the top three shooters,

Though many top-level shooters opt for over-under shotguns, some like their favorite semi-automatics. This is Tim Murphy of Kansas on his way to a very high score at the 1990 USSCA National shoot with a Beretta 303.

Young shooters can have a great time at sporting clays. This youngster is shoot-ing a semi-automatic that will help reduce the amount of recoil.

legendary Dan Carlisle of California and Kansas's Tim Murphy, were shooting Beretta automatics. Their scores and their guns raised a lot of eyebrows—particularly of those who'd spent twice as much for a gun but only shot half as well.

The problem of jamming is one complaint many people have about automatics. It seems like some brands are more susceptible than others. The type of ammo can also make a difference, as can cleaning and upkeep. You can bet experts like Carlisle and Murphy keep their automatics in tip-top condition.

Without a doubt, the pump shotgun is the rarest of the four major actions on a sporting clays course. Though very affordable and popular in the field, the time and energy it takes to work the action on a pump can be a problem in sporting clays. That's not to say it's impossible to get a good score with a Remington 870 or a Browning BP5, it's just a little more difficult. But if you're shooting strictly for pleasure, you should shoot whatever you want, be it a $25,000 Beretta or a $200 pawnshop Mossberg. The main thing is to have fun.

BARRELS

The last decade or so has seen some changes in the way American shooters think about shotgun barrel length. For years it was believed that there was a strong correlation between barrel length and downrange killing power. Many hunters relied on thirty- and thirty-two-inch barrels to give them added power for long-range waterfowling.

Then it was learned that choke, not barrel length, was the true deciding factor in how well a gun would perform on long shots. Almost instantaneously we began to see shorter shotgun barrels as hunters took advantage of their easier handling and lighter weight. The twenty-six-inch barrel, traditionally used only in short-range sports such as bob-white, woodcock, and ruffed grouse hunting, is now probably the most popular length on hunting fields. Barrels even as short as twenty-one inches aren't uncommon.

With the phenomenal growth of sporting clays, however, came a renewed demand for longer shotgun barrels. Why, some would ask, would you want a long barrel for a sport that often demands breaking quick targets at relatively short ranges? There are a variety of reasons. A longer sight plane is very important to trap shooters and can be of a slighter advantage to sporting clays shooters. Also, the added weight of a long barrel can help reduce recoil by a small degree. Plus the longer barrels help control muzzle jump, which is important in doubles shooting.

But what's probably most important is that a long barrel swings more smoothly and consistently than a shorter one. Once you get a thirty-inch over-under moving, it just seems to carry itself along. Since you already have the gun pointed roughly where you'll be shooting the target, the extra barrel length is of little bother—at least not compared with using it to turn and take a shot at a rooster pheasant that's flushed behind you in the uplands.

You'll see a variety of barrel lengths on a sporting clays course. Local hunters out for a little fun and practice will probably be toting their favorite bird guns. Those who are a little more serious about sporting clays will probably be gunning with a barrel that's between twenty-eight and thirty-two inches. Generally, the larger or more experienced the shooter, the longer the barrels. The thirty-inch barrel is growing in popularity. Many who like to use their clays guns while hunting will opt for the twenty-eight-inch barrel. It's a length that works well both on a course and in the field.

RIBS

It's extremely rare to see a nice shotgun without some sort of flat sight plane over its barrel or barrels. In fact, ribs on shotgun barrels are so common that most of the debate now centers on style rather than need. Shooters have a variety of ribs to choose from, with the variables being height and width. The good old standard rib basically extends straight out from over the breech and parallels the barrel all the way to the muzzle. This rib is usually about five-sixteenths-inch wide.

Wider ribs are designed to give the shooter a wider, more comfortable sight plane and can help those who cant the gun. There's also the step-rib, which angles up before leveling off and paralleling the barrel. Those who like step-ribs claim the added height makes it easier to get a good, level look down the barrel.

Beads are often placed at the end of the rib and about halfway back on the barrel. A single bead at the muzzle can supposedly act like a sight. A two-bead setup is sometimes sold on the premise that the shooter can line the pair up in such a way as to guarantee he'll be getting the proper sight picture.

It's worth noting, however, that there are a lot of really fine shooters and shooting instructors who think that too much emphasis is being placed on rib styles and bead configurations for sporting clays. There's no question that ribs and beads can help in shotgun sports in which the shooter gets to aim and look down the barrel before he even sees or calls for the bird. But such isn't the case in sporting clays, where the shooter gives almost his full attention to the flying target. As in upland bird hunting, the gun seems to come up on its own, and the shooter fires when the muzzle is in the right place. Most of the time you're not even aware of the rib and whether or not it has a bead on it.

Basically, if the gun fits the shooter, the muzzle is going to be pointing right where he wants it. If the gun fit is way off, the time it takes to mentally line things up is drastically going to hurt the shooter's chances of breaking the target.

For the most part, if a sporting clays shooter is having trouble breaking targets, no single piece of equipment (except maybe the gun, by being fitted to the shooter's body) is going to instantly turn him into an 80 percent shooter. If there were such an item, I'd have bought it long ago. As much as it hurts to admit it, when I miss a target, the fault is totally mine and nothing can change that.

MODIFICATIONS

As with just about any piece of equipment, there are a number of modifications that can be made to a sporting clays gun. These may or may not have bona fide concepts. What should and shouldn't be added to a gun is up to the individual, depending upon his taste and problems. It would be very easy for a person to spend hundreds of dollars on such additions. Maybe they'll make him a better shooter and maybe not. Most avid shooters advise that you proceed with caution when considering a modification and, if possible, do some test firing with a gun that's already been modified in that direction.

Recoil Reduction

There's no debating the fact that a sporting clays gun is going to kick. Given the nature of the sport, in which you'll often fire fifty, one hundred, or even more shells a day, that recoil can have an adverse effect on your body. One of the first things to consider is whether your gun's amount of recoil is normal or excessive. Also, observe where the gun is kicking your body. If it's any place other than the "pocket" of your shoulder, for example your cheek or arm, you're using a gun that simply doesn't fit. A stock that's too long or short or a comb that's too high or low will definitely beat the shooter up some.

But even those whose guns fit properly will usually want to keep recoil to a minimum. One way is through shell selection. (Details on shells are given in chapter 10.) Another alternative is to trade the over-under in on a quality semiautomatic and let the gun's action use some of the recoil.

There's also the ever-popular recoil pad, a soft but firm pad of rubber or leather that absorbs some of the gun's recoil. A few shooters rely on slip-on pads, which slide over the gun's stock. Most, however, have their pads professionally mounted. For one thing, they look much better. Also, a gunsmith can remove enough of the stock that the gun still fits well once the pad is added.

One thing to keep in mind when shopping for a recoil pad is the importance of a smooth surface. Sporting clays requires a smooth, snagfree gun mount. There are some pads on the market that seem to snag on a vest or shirt like Velcro. If your pad catches on your clothing, you may need to have your stock shortened. If the gun fits but still hangs up, a little black, vinyl electricians' tape can be used to smooth things up.

Recoil-reducing systems can also be added to a gun, primarily in the stock. The basic concept is to add more weight to lessen the thrust of a gun's kick. Specially made cylinders of mercury both add weight and prolong the recoil, thereby taking the sharp edge off a gun's kick. Some say it makes the recoil more of a shove than a sharp punch.

Do they work? Yes. Do you need one in your gun? It all depends on how much recoil you can tolerate. If recoil doesn't bother you, the answer is obvious. But one thing is for sure—if you're flinching like a toad in a hailstorm every time you pull the trigger, something is going to have to be done or your scores and your shooting enjoyment will plummet.

Trigger Adjustments

Some guns come with triggers that can be adjusted up or down and back or forth for comfort. Wide or narrow, high or low, it's all a matter of personal preference.

One aspect of triggers that doesn't get much attention is the amount of pull it takes to fire the gun. Most sporting clays guns feature crisp triggers that snap at about three to four pounds of pressure. Most

This shooter has added a little moleskin to the stock of his gun in hopes of getting a better gun fit and possible a slight reduction in recoil to the face. The best method by far is to get a try-gun fitting and have the gun's stock bent accordingly.

shooters don't like a lot of creep or pressure when they're firing. When it's time to break a target, the less effort it takes, the better. Also, the harder you have to yank on a trigger, the more apt you are to flinch at the shot.

On the other hand, you don't want a trigger that's set so light that you have to worry about tripping it before you're ready to make the shot. If you're having problems, a competent gunsmith can get your trigger snapping exactly the way you want it.

Comb Adjustments

There are many ways to work with a comb to get the gun shooting where it should. For years shooters have added a little patch of mole-skin to raise the stock a little. Some have attacked the stock of their favorite target gun with a sheet of sandpaper until they've gotten the comb down to where they wanted it. Others have sent the stock in and had an adjustable comb installed. (Basically, we're talking about a poor man's try-gun, with a stock that can be adjusted up and down and maybe from side to side.)

Some people refuse to use adjustable combs because, frankly, they look pretty unattractive. There's also the problem of knowing how to adjust one to get the most out of it. To be honest, that's something many shooters can't do well. It can also be tough to leave well enough alone. I've been at shoots where a frustrated shooter has walked away from a station, pulled a wrench from his pocket, and literally attacked an adjustable stock. A few stations later, he went through round two with the gun. There's no way that gun could have fit him or have been shooting where it was supposed to by the time he got done with it.

If you take the adjustable-comb road, you should consider going to an experienced gun fitter, getting the gun adjusted to your body, and then throwing away the wrench. But if you go to that much trouble, you might as well get a try-gun fit and have your existing stock altered.

Back-Boring

Those who get a barrel back-bored are basically getting it opened up a little. It's hoped that by having had the barrel reamed from the forcing cone to the choke, the gun will offer less resistance to the wad and shot. Less damage to shot, higher velocity, and reduced recoil are the desired effects.

Like any gun alterations, the effectiveness of back-boring is debat-able and no doubt will vary from gun to gun. There also seems to be a fine line between "just right" and too much boring. If a barrel is opened too much, inconsistent pressure and velocity can be a problem. Though great in concept, back-boring may not always be the ticket to better shooting. It may produce a gun that is fickle about brands of shells or that must be reloaded to perform properly.

Lengthening the Forcing Cone

For those who don't know, the forcing cone is the tapered part of the barrel just in front of the shell chamber, whose function is to ease the shot's transition from the shell to the slightly smaller barrel. As the name implies, it's a cone that forces the shot into the barrel.

Some shooters have their forcing cones lengthened, adding more taper to it to ease the pressure on the shot as it goes into the barrel. Most newer guns, however, already have a relatively long forcing cone. The advantage to having a long forcing cone is that the lower peak pressure means the shot will be less deformed, and it will fly truer and deliver better patterns. Some say the process also reduces a gun's felt recoil.

Barrel Porting

Ports are small slits or holes just before the barrel meets the choke, designed to let a little of the pressure off the shot string before it goes through the choke. If all goes as planned, the decrease in pressure will keep the shot from becoming deformed and give the shooter a better pattern. It's also hoped that the ports will blow the pressure of the powder in a desired direction, meaning less felt recoil to the shooter and less muzzle jump.

Disadvantages include a significant increase in the gun's noise level, and the ports may allow pieces of burnt powder to escape and possibly be blown back into the face of the shooter. In addition, ports must be kept clean.

There are enough ported guns around that it shouldn't be hard to find one to test-fire before having your favorite sporting clays gun altered.

11

TRY A
TRY-GUN

Mark Moxley's first experiences with sporting clays weren't very happy. In fact, he considered them downright dismal.

An enthusiastic quail hunter, Moxley said he went into sporting clays figuring he'd be able to bust clay targets with the same proficiency he did bobwhites. He didn't. "I was extremely discouraged the first few times," said Moxley. "I was shooting about 45 to 50 percent. That's great for some, but I knew I should have been doing better. I was pretty down on myself."

Then one day his scores suddenly jumped to 65 percent. Now he's justifiably proud of his 75 to 80 percent average. What did Moxley do to bring on such an impressive improvement? He finally fixed the blame where it belonged—his gun. Then he and Michael Murphy did something about it.

"Murphy proved to me that the gun really didn't fit me," said Moxley. "He also got me into one that did. The difference was like night and day when I shot. My scores went up immediately. It was the fit that did it."

Trap, skeet, and wing shooters alike have talked about the importance of gun fit for decades. But in none of these sports is it as important to success as in the game of sporting clays.

"Sporting clays is an instinctual kind of shooting," says Keith Lupton, Sandonona Shooting School, Millbrook, New York. "It's important that the gun fit the shooter because there isn't time to adjust yourself to the dimensions of the gun like in trap or skeet. In sporting clays when the gun goes up it must be pointing exactly where you're looking or you simply can't shoot well."

Most guns are designed to fit "Mr. Average," a person about five feet ten inches and 160 pounds. "Obviously most people aren't built like that," explains Lupton. "They usually need some adjustments."

For years American shooters have guessed at such adjustments, maybe shaving a little wood or adding a thin pad of moleskin. But as with all guesswork, the results were minimal at best.

There was no guesswork involved when the frustrated Moxley took his problems to Murphy, an Augusta, Kansas, fine gun and sporting clays accessory dealer. Amid the hundreds of nice shotguns that line Murphy's shop sits a pair, one an over-under and the other a side-by-side, that feel slightly awkward and stock-heavy.

They are "try-guns," and thanks to a variety of joints and extensions they allow a trained gun fitter like Murphy to learn a shooter's specific stock dimensions.

The first step to the fitting is simply finding the shooter's dominant eye, sometimes called the "shooting eye." Using an exercise in which the shooter forms a small circle with his outstretched hands, focusing on an object, then pulling his hands back while keeping the object centered, Murphy can quickly tell whether the person should be shooting right- or left-handed.

With that determined, he hands his client the try-gun, showing him that snap-caps have been installed, and then points to the shooter's imaginary target—Murphy's nose.

"The only real way to know what the shooter is seeing is to be looking right down the barrel at him," said Murphy. "You can't look over his shoulder or simply go by what he tells you. I'm actually sighting in the try-gun from the muzzle end. My target is to get the iris of the shooter's eye floating at the other end of the gun barrel."

To insure the shooter doesn't fit his body to the try-gun, Murphy

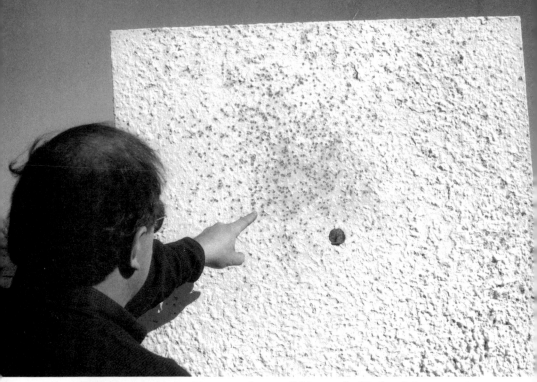

This shooter was checking to see how well his gun fit. He faced the patterning board, snapped the gun into position and fired as soon as the stock hit his cheek. Obviously he's shooting high and to the left.

instructs him to take a solid shooting stance, gun at ready, while focusing his gaze on Murphy's nose. "Remember where my nose is, then close your eyes without moving your head. Then snap the gun up and point it where you think my nose is."

After a few such mounts the fitter will know what has to be done to sculpt the try-gun to the shooter's body. Using the gun's movable comb, Murphy first adjusts the gun for drop at comb and then heel. An inward extension allows the fitter to adjust the gun's length of pull. Cast is adjusted with a joint at the gun's grip, which moves the stock from side to side. It's a process that takes a surprising amount of time because, according to Murphy, "there's no such thing as 'close enough.'"

"What some people consider to be only a fraction of an inch can make a big, big difference in how well they shoot a gun," Murphy emphasizes. "If your drop at comb measurement is off a quarter inch with a thirty-inch barrel, your pattern will be off close to ten inches at forty yards. Even that doesn't sound like much, but it will have you shooting at targets with the fringe of your pattern. That also leaves precious little room for error in your shooting."

Eventually the try-gun will be adjusted so that it is almost an extension of the shooter's body. No matter where the shooter is looking, the gun will be pointing right there when the gun is shouldered. Still, the fitting is only half over.

The joint in the grip, adjustable cheek and stock length of this try-gun lets a good gunfitter mold the shotgun to fit a shooter's body. Once the precise measurements are known the shooter's clays gun can be adjusted.

This gun fits the shooter's face perfectly. Note how the stock nestles right into his cheek and how his eyes are looking right down the barrel.

Both Lupton and Murphy agree that the only true way to get an accurate fit is to do a "shooting-fit." "Some people will hold the gun differently when they know they're not shooting," says Murphy. "Often they'll tense up a little in anticipation of recoil. Regardless, in *every case* we've had to change the gun a little from the in-store fit."

Standing thirty yards from a patterning board, the shooter replaces the try-gun's snap-caps with a single 2½-inch shotshell. The gunner takes a shooting stance, concentrates on the center of the board, snaps the gun to his shoulder, and fires as soon as his cheek hits the gun's comb.

In most cases the fitter will inspect the patterning board by himself. In Murphy's case he'll be able to see the pattern smack the fresh white paint on his metal patterning board, but he'll refrain from informing the shooter of the exact location of the impact.

"It's important that the shooter not know where his pattern is going," Murphy says. "If he knows he's shooting high and to the left, he may subconsciously try to adjust the point of impact. I also want his full concentration on the center of the patterning board."

Final adjustments will be made and eventually the shooter will be putting load after load where Murphy wants them: dead center (rather than a little high as trap and skeet shooters prefer). "In sporting clays we're almost always shooting at a target that is falling or slowing in speed," explains Murphy. "In the past a lot of people wanted about 70 percent of their pattern going high. For a sporting clays gun I want it fifty-fifty."

Once he is confident the try-gun fit is proper, the fitter will have the measurements that fit the shooter's body as well as a tailored suit.

While some shooters will opt to buy a new gun with a customized stock, most simply get their favorite clays gun altered. Spacers can be added between the gun stock and pad to extend the length of pull. Drop at comb or heel and cast can be altered with a hot oil bend that won't mar the gun's looks.

Sometimes the changes are minimal. Often it's one-eighth inch either way at the drop at comb, or lengthening or shortening a stock by an inch or less. Other times it will take major reconstructive surgery to get a shooter's gun to fit his body.

In one case Murphy had a six-foot-five-inch client who was struggling to bust 20 percent on the clays course. The dominant eye test showed that the shooter should be using his left rather than his right shoulder.

Not surprisingly, the shooter had been using a stock that was well short of what his long body needed. An inch and a half was added to length of pull and the drop at comb was also adjusted. Thanks to the fitting and a few lessons, the shooter's scores tripled!

In a few cases, Murphy admits, a try-gun fitting and stock alteration has only added a couple broken targets to a shooter's score. "But those are usually really good shooters," he says. "For them that's a significant improvement." For a serious tournament shooter that can mean the difference between a trophy and an "almost."

But most experienced shooters see a 10 to 20 percent improvement on their scores. That's enough to make the cost and effort worthwhile. As Murphy says, "With all of the fittings I've done, I've never had anyone ask for his money back."

TRY-GUN TERMINOLOGY

Drop at comb. The most important of all the dimensions. The drop at comb is the distance between the line of sight down the barrel and the front portion of the comb. It controls the vertical aspect of shooting: If a gun's drop at comb is too low, the shooter is going to look out over the end of the barrel and shoot high.

Cast. The amount of horizontal bend in the gun's stock. A bend to the right is cast off, a bend to the left is cast on. An improper cast is often to blame when a shooter consistently shoots to the left or right. The shooter's eye is like the rear sight on a rifle. If the cast isn't right, the eye won't be looking perfectly down the barrel.

Drop at heel. The distance from the line of sight down the barrel to the top of the heel of the gun. It affects if a shooter will shoot high or low and is usually just a fine adjustment for the drop at comb.

Pitch. The angle of the butt compared to the line of sight. It is very important in determining the angle of a mounted gun. If there is too much pitch, the gun will often kick up on the shooter's shoulder and the shot could go low. Pitch isn't much of a problem for most shooters, but it can be important for barrel-chested men and women because of the size of their chests.

Length of pull. The distance from the gun's trigger to the center of the butt. Very important for optimum comfort. "If the length of pull is too short, the shooter's face will be placed too far up the stock and he may hit his nose with his hand upon recoil," said Murphy. "If the length of pull is too long, the shooter may end up mounting the gun on the edge of his shoulder or arm. That can cause a great deal of discomfort and the shots will go to the left for a right-handed shooter."

Michael Murphy demonstrates a gun that fits him well: his eye is looking right down the gun's rib. When this occurs the gun should automatically shoot right where the eye is looking.

TROUBLESHOOTING
The following are some indications of a poorly fitting gun:

- Continually missing or barely chipping easy, eye-level, going-away shots. This is a prime example of a shotgun not shooting where the shooter is looking.

- Inconsistency in angling targets. For example, rarely missing targets curving to the left but seldom busting those that head to the right. This is a good indication that the shooter's pattern is flying to the left.

- Discomfort to the face, shoulder, or arm after shooting. A properly fitted gun will easily nestle into the "pocket" of the shoulder and the hand won't slap the face at recoil.

An excellent way to test your gun is to draw a small, fist-sized black circle on patterning paper or board and set it at eye level thirty yards away. Start with the gun low and shoot the target soon after the butt hits the shoulder. Be careful not to aim the shotgun like a rifle. Repeat the test several times until you find where the gun is consistently shooting.

————————— 12 —————————

ALL CHOKED UP

No matter how long it is or how many ways it's been modified, the most important part of a shotgun barrel lies within its last few inches. It's the gun's choke that most determines how a load of pellets will perform once it leaves the muzzle.

In the most basic terms, a gun's choke is the amount of restriction near the muzzle. Contrary to popular belief, the length of the barrel has no effect on the size of the pattern. Any choke at all will squeeze the shot string down to a smaller diameter.

For decades guns came with a single restriction. Those who wanted greater variety would have to get a second gun or at least an extra barrel or set of barrels. Then, with the advent of threaded choke barrels that come with a whole set of screw-in chokes, a hunter or sporting clays shooter could gun the gamut of shooting ranges. With a skeet choke, a gun could be lethal on fifteen-yard targets or woodcocks. Choked with a full tube, that same gun could cleanly fold a rooster pheasant at fifty yards.

Yet all is not really as simple as it seems in the world of shotgun chokes. We're not dealing with an exact science. There can be a world of differences from gun to gun, from barrel to barrel, and from tube to

98

Most sporting clays shooters opt for the versatility of a gun with screw-in choke types. This shooter is adding a modified tube in preparation for a long crossing shot.

tube. Also, things aren't always what they seem; for example, though they're usually fairly accurate, not all fixed-choke barrels shoot as they're marked.

A few years ago I got a great deal on a sweet, little 20-gauge side-by-side. Weighing just five and one-half pounds, with a fix-choked improved cylinder and modified, this gun seemed perfect for grasslands quail and for playing around with a few clays. But I was surprised at how often I missed close shots at both birds and targets. Then one day I got a thirty-yard shot at a crossing cottontail. At the shot, I centered the rabbit in a cloud of dust that wasn't much bigger than a large pizza.

I took the gun to Michael Murphy before the next season to get a true reading on how the gun was choked. My sweet, little scattergun was choked with the equivalent of full and extra-full! Since then I've seen Murphy check many guns, and though my 20 gauge was the farthest from the norm, I've been surprised at how many guns were not what they were labeled.

To totally understand chokes, it helps to first understand barrel and choke restrictions. As stated earlier, there is no exact standard for barrels or chokes. Though .729 of an inch is the standard inside diameter for an American 12 gauge, not all companies adhere to that exact measurement. Some barrels may be .010 (ten thousandths of an inch) larger, and it will take more restriction to get a .739 barrel to shoot like a .729 barrel.

It's for that reason that most avid shooters and gun experts talk restriction differences when the topic is chokes. For example, if the barrel diameter is .730 and the choke is .715, the difference will be .015. The choke will also be .015. The greater the constriction (the higher the number), the tighter the choke and the pattern as it leaves the muzzle and as it flies downrange.

How do you get an accurate reading of the inside of a barrel and choke? With a bore micrometer, a neat little tool that has a dial at one end of a rod and a probe at the other. The probe is lowered to the middle of the barrel and the rod is raised, and a needle on the dial will measure the amount of constriction as soon as the probe enters the choke. (A bore micrometer can also be used to check for dents, pits, and other irregularities.)

Though the bore micrometer can be a lot of fun to tinker with, its price of several hundred dollars puts it out of reach for many shooters. Most good gunsmiths and fine gun dealers have the tool, however, and don't mind measuring guns for good customers.

Those who don't have access to a bore micrometer can figure their chokes the old-fashioned way, by shooting them at a patterning board, taking forty-yard shots at a thirty-inch circle. Divide the number of pellets inside the circle by the total number of pellets, and you'll have a percentage. (It works well to shoot the pattern and then draw the circle so the circle is centered.) For example, if there are 274 pellets in the circle and 392 pellets overall, 392 into 274 would be roughly .70. Using the chart at the end of this chapter, look up that percentage and, voila, you know you have a full choke.

Please keep in mind that different shells will perform differently

A patterning board is the real proving ground for a shotgun. Here Michael Murphy paints his metal "board" in preparation for checking a shotgun's point of impact. The gun's pattern will easily show on the fresh paint.

out of the same choke. Plated and extra-hard shot will have a tighter pattern than softer shot. A shell with a simple, round disc for a wad will throw a more open pattern than one that has a wad with an extended sleeve or "fingers" to hold the shot together longer.

Surprisingly, identical chokes may sometimes throw significantly different patterns. Though two Beretta improved cylinder chokes may both measure .010, their patterns may not be the same. You'll also sometimes find that one choke may throw different patterns with shells that appear to be totally alike. A load of Winchesters may pattern differently than a similar load of Federals. Why? There's a wide range of possibilities, but no one knows for sure.

The important thing to remember is that not all chokes are alike. Each takes a little experimentation and tinkering to determine what load will produce the best results, and that can be part of the fun.

Chokes generally shoot tighter with larger shot. A shooter can split choke sizes by changing shot size or shell velocity.

It's also important to balance range and pellet size and count with a specific choke. Generally, the more open the choke, the smaller the size of shot needed to adequately fill the entire pattern. And it's feasible that a target could fly through a pattern unscathed if there aren't enough pellets. For example, a skeet choke loaded with one ounce of 7½ shot could have some gaping holes at forty yards. I have enough trouble hitting a midi at that range; the last thing I need is to have the target slide through a gap in my pattern.

Downrange breaking power is another consideration. A modified choke with number 9 shot might give a nice pattern at forty-five yards, but the pellets may not have enough energy to break a tough target. A few 7½ pellets definitely will.

The table below gives some specifics on chokes, including constrictions, percentages at forty yards, optimum shot sizes for sporting clays, and ranges. All of the figures are given for 12 gauges and are approximations.

SKEET I	.001–.004	45%	#8 & #9	to 30 yds.

The skeet I choke is an excellent target choke, usually giving a nice, even pattern.

IMPROVED CYLINDER	.005–.014	50%	#7½–#9	20–35 yds.

The improved cylinder is probably the most all-around choke in sporting clays. Uniform patterns and the ability to deliver well with all sizes of shot make it extremely popular with novices and experts alike.

SKEET II	.008–.013	55%	#7½–#9	25–35 yds.

Skeet II has long been a popular hunting choke in double-barrels. On the average it patterns a little tighter than an improved cylinder.

MODIFIED	.015–.023	60%	#7½	30–40 yds.

The modified is usually the tightest choke needed on a sporting clays course and then only sparingly. The tight pattern can be a hindrance to beginning shooters. Some loads will develop a core density (a cluster of pellets near the center of the pattern).

| IMPROVED MODIFIED | .023–.029 | 65% | #7½ | 35–45 yds. |

Originally named as an improvement on the modified choke, this choke falls in between modified and full. It's usually of little use on most sporting clays course. Core density can be a problem if you're not centering the target in your pattern.

| FULL | .030–.040 | 70% | #7½ | 40–50 yds. |

Since few clays courses torture their clients with fifty-yard targets, the full choke is seldom used in the sport. It can, however, be fun to play with when not in competition. If you're busting targets with a full choke, everything must be synchronized. A full choke will also let you know if you're just chipping the backs of the targets.

THE
SHELL GAME

The shooter and the gun he shoots are no better than the shells he loads it with. People who've spent much time sniping at targets and patterning boards will guarantee you that the proper shells can make a big difference.

It helps to understand the basic chemistry of a shell. Though it's only a millisecond from the time you pull the trigger until either the target breaks or you start making excuses, the shell goes through an amazing number of changes. First the firing pin strikes the primer, and it explodes like a cap and ignites the powder, which burns (not explodes) quickly. The pressure from the burning powder pushes on the wad, which pushes the shot out of the shell case and down the barrel.

SHOT

Actually, the powder and the wad have a fairly easy time of it. The shot, on the other hand, gets a triple whammy. The first shock is when the powder ignites and the pellets at the top of the shot column get a severe case of whiplash as they're rear-ended by the lower pellets and the wad. The next crunch is when the pellets go from the chamber into the smaller forcing cone. Pressures are increased yet again when the shot column has to narrow to go through the choke.

Such pressures can have a tremendous effect on a metal as soft as lead. Some pellets can develop flat spots. Anyone who's tried to throw a lopsided softball will tell you that such an irregular object won't fly true. Many ammo companies harden their shot pellets by adding antimony. The higher the percentage of antimony, the harder the shot and the better it will retain its shape and a good pattern. Shot that's plated with copper or other metals will also remain truer.

Most sporting clays courses limit their shooters to $1^{1}/8$ ounces of shot that's no larger than $7^{1}/2$ and no smaller than 9. Such limitations are absolutely no hindrance—with the three common sizes of $7^{1}/2$, 8, and 9, there's not a target that can't be broken from ten to fifty yards. If you can hit it, the pellets will do the rest.

As briefly covered in the chapter on chokes, there are advantages and disadvantages to every size of shot. The $7^{1}/2$s have the greatest downrange breaking power, but you get fewer pellets per ounce than with, say, a load of 9s. And though number 9s don't perform well on long shots, they have more pellets, which will spread farther and faster then with the other sizes.

The quantity of pellets in a shell should also be considered. At first thought, it might seem like the more pellets, the better. A load with $1^{1}/8$ ounces will usually have a slightly larger and denser pattern than a shell with less shot. But given an equal amount of powder, the heavier load is going to shoot considerably more slowly. If you lessen the amount of shot to pick up a little added velocity, you may start breaking those fast targets you've been shooting a few inches behind.

Also, in some chokes, a 1-ounce load will pattern better than a $1^{1}/8$-ounce load. The added pellets aren't worth the sacrifice of speed if they're going to fly about in different directions.

There's also the little matter of recoil to consider. The heavier the load, the more resistance it offers the power of the powder, and the more the load will recoil.

POWDER

You get into a similar more-versus-less debate when it comes to powder. Again, a lot of shooters will instantly zero in on the $3^{1}/4$ drams that's the maximum allowed at most courses. But anyone who's ever shot fifty to one hundred of those shells can attest to their recoil. A lot of shooters prefer the lighter-kicking 3-dram load. Some recoil-sensitive shooters even drop down to the mild $2^3/4$-dram load.

Those worried about losing velocity can use a smaller load of shot, or they can drop down to a smaller shot size so that they'll still have an equal number of pellets. For example, a load with 3 drams of powder and 1 ounce of number 8s in some ways compares favorably with a load of $3^1/4$ drams of powder and $1^1/8$ ounces of $7^1/2$s, though you do, of course, lose some breaking power on really long sporting clays shots.

As you reduce the powder drams on a given load of shot, the pattern will usually tighten up. So a shooter who wants to tighten up his pattern downrange can, for example, drop from a $3^1/4$-dram, $1^1/8$-ounce load of number 8s to $2^3/4$ drams and $1^1/8$ ounce of number 8s. He will, however, need to increase his lead slightly.

The only way to make such decisions is through trial and error on both a patterning board and a sporting clays course.

---------------------------------- 14 ----------------------------------

ACCESSORIES

From time to time you will see a first-time shooter head out onto a local course carrying no more than his gun, a couple of boxes of shells, and a mind full of questions. On successive trips you'll see that same person starting to reverse things a bit—he'll have fewer and fewer questions, but he'll be carrying more and more besides his shotgun and ammo.

As with all sports, the sporting clays market is full of accessories. Some actually help the gunner improve his score. Others are items of convenience and comfort that help the shooter reap more enjoyment from the sport. Still others neither help nor offer added pleasure—that is, unless you're the company that's selling them.

HATS

The style of a person's hat, like a lot of clothing, seems to be an expression of his or her personality. Sporting clays headgear is no exception. At a big shoot, you'll see expensive cowboy hats and promo ball caps (probably the most popular) and everything in between.

A good hat can keep your head cool or warm and help keep the sun out of your eyes. Get whatever feels best, but make sure it won't obstruct your vision when you're shooting.

Shooting Vests

Probably no piece of clothing is as unique to sporting clays as a good vest that's been designed for the sport. Unlike trap and skeet, in which the gun is premounted, this sport's need for a smooth and consistent mount calls for a special kind of shoulder covering.

First of all, a shooting vest has to fit the upper chest well. A loose-fitting vest can buckle and/or slip, causing the gun to hang up as it's being mounted. The fabric or covering on the shooting shoulder should be smooth as silk. A lot of experienced sporting clays shooters mount the gun by sliding it from under the arm up onto the shoulder because the less the gun butt has to leave the body, the less there is that can go wrong. The combination of a smooth butt or recoil pad and a slick material on the shoulder helps make a good gun mount almost automatic.

What a vest is like below the shoulder area is up to the shooter. Most will fit rather snugly but aren't so tight as to be uncomfortable or hot. Sporting clays vests come with a wide variety of pockets and compartments, as some shooters like to carry everything right on their body: shells, spare chokes, glasses, lenses, hearing protectors, sun protection . . .

Tote Bags

Rather than carry everything in the vest and subject themselves to the constant weight and restriction, many shooters opt to carry their shells and accessories in a small tote bag. It's a lot easier to shoot a station when you leave the weight of the ammo and accessories resting on the ground.

I've seen some shooters invest in specially made bags with compartments designed for nearly every need. I've also seen shooters simply pile all of their goodies in an old, cheap plastic or leather gym bag. The targets they shot at didn't seem too concerned about what they were carrying.

Shoes

There doesn't seem to be a shoe made especially for sporting clays, like there is for baseball or golf. Shooters should try to find something that is comfortable and allows the wearer to pivot freely on the ball of the foot. Most shooters who think about it prefer a shoe that's higher in the heel so they'll automatically be up on the balls of their feet. Such shoes seem to make it easier to get into a proper shooting stance and can help reduce recoil to a small degree.

The soles of the shoes should have enough traction to allow a shooter to get around easily and safely on a clays course (slick soles can be a tremendous problem on wet, muddy, and/or hilly courses). On the other hand, you don't want a sole that digs too deeply into the ground. There are times in sporting clays when having your feet immobile could be a big disadvantage.

Shooting Gloves

Some shooters like to wear a pair of thin, leather shooting gloves. As in golfing and baseball, the main advantage of gloves is that they give you a better grip and thus better control. They also allow your hands to absorb a little of the gun's recoil. Gloves can also help you maintain a good grip even once your gun's barrels have gotten hot from prolonged shooting.

Pants

The most important thing to look for in a pair of sporting clays pants is that they be loose fitting and comfortable. In the heat of the summer, a lot of gunners opt for shorts.

Shirts

As with pants, comfort is the main thing. Try to pick a shirt that's nonbinding. Those who are shooting without a vest will want to take extra care to wear a shirt that will allow for a smooth, snagfree gun mount.

Clothing for Bad Weather

A shooter will occasionally face an unusually cold or wet day on the course. Possibly the best alternative is to slip a large coat on over the shooting vest and then remove the bulky garment just before you step into the shooting station. There's a definite correlation between wearing too much and getting lower-than-normal scores. The more your mount and swing are restricted, the less effective you'll be on a course.

Cold fingers are usually best left in the warmth of pockets or in mittens that can be removed prior to the shot. Since sporting clays is a sport of pure enjoyment, few shooters will venture out in much of a rain. Those who do usually carry small umbrellas or wear very thin raingear.

OTHER ITEMS

You'll find an almost endless variety of things being carried on sporting clays courses across America. A lot of shooters have "shooting towels" clipped to their belts. Their main purpose is for wiping sweat and dirt from hands and faces, though I usually have to use mine to wipe away tears after I see my final score!

Since guns generally feature screw-in chokes, most sporting clays shooters will be carrying an assortment of related items including, of course, extra chokes. Probably the most popular tubes are skeet, improved cylinder, and modified. Many over-under and side-by-side shooters carry pairs of both skeet and improved cylinder chokes so they can equip both barrels with the same choke if needed. Specially made cases make carrying and choosing chokes much easier.

Of course, a set of chokes won't be of any use if you don't take along a wrench. Changing chokes is never time-consuming, even with the primitive wrenches most manufacturers supply with their choke systems, but shooters who want to make the chore even faster and easier can use speed wrenches, some of which work similarly to power screwdrivers.

Also, don't forget to lug an extra box of assorted ammo. One station may require something a little heavier than the light load of 8s you're carrying. It's also quite possible that you may need a few more shells than there are targets, for example, if you shoot at an irregular bird before the judge can make the call and offer you another target.

Such items as insect repellent and sunscreen can help keep pleasurable outings that way. A small bottle of water and a light snack will help you maintain your body at its shooting peak. And pencils and pens always have a way of breaking when you're the farthest from headquarters, so take a spare or two.

In fact, it's not a bad idea to carry a spare of just about anything you take with you on the field. Sooner or later you or someone in your group will come up missing a hearing protector or a pair of shooting glasses. Speaking of glasses, it's tough to hit what you can't see, so take something to clean dirty lenses.

And what about . . .

THE EYES
HAVE IT

Many sporting clays courses require gunners to wear shooting glasses as a safety precaution. Rightfully so—a pair of shatterproof lenses can protect the eyes against stray pellets, gun malfunctions, or pieces of falling targets.

But there's another important reason for wearing shooting glasses: performance! Simply put, the right shooting glasses can and will raise your sporting clays score.

Unlike traditional sunglasses, which darken surroundings and soothe the eye, most sporting clays shooting glasses are designed to bring the shooter's vision to its top performance. "The key is to bring the target out from its surroundings," says Bud Decot, owner of Decot Hy-Wyd Inc., a top-of-the-line shooting glasses manufacturer. "The quicker you can pick it up with your eyes, focus on it, and continue to see it clearly, the better your chances of breaking it."

Decot, probably America's top authority on the subject, explained the reason for bright-tinted glasses for optimum success. Like the aperature of a camera, the eye picks up the best definition and depth of field when the pupil is constricted. Target color and the surrounding background can play an important role in how well a pair of shooting

A good pair of shooting glasses can improve a shooter's seeing ability and offer needed protection.

glasses will perform. "It's important to use lenses of a color that will best isolate the color of the target," Decot advises. "For example, if a shooter is trying to pinpoint a standard orange target coming out of green treetops, he'll want to use lenses that accent the orange but mellow the green.

So what lens colors are the best? Like many aspects of shooting, that's a question that has no true answer, because no two people see all colors the same way. A shooter's lifestyle can also have a major impact on how well he can see. According to Decot, excessive amounts of nicotine and alcohol can cause eyes to become light sensitive. A two-pack-a-day smoker, he said, will often be forced to use darker glasses than a nonsmoking shooter. Also, a gunner who spends much of his time inside and/or wearing dark sunglasses can initially have problems wearing brightly tinted lenses.

Decot can, however, recommend a few popular shades for consideration. "Target Orange" lenses will do an excellent job of enhancing the orange tops of many clay targets. It's possibly the most popular color on the market. "Target Sun" is actually a purple tint that dampens green colors and enhances orange targets against a green background. An excellent choice for spring and summer gunning in the trees, it is also extremely helpful on courses where the targets come out of pine trees. A good number of shooters continue to rely on the traditional yellow and gold lenses to bring in as much light as possible. These are an invaluable asset on cloudy and foggy days.

One of the most important aspects, according to Decot, is wearing the brightest tint that the shooter's eye can tolerate for maximum pupil constriction. He adds that the eyes can be trained to tolerate a tint that may seem too bright at first.

It's important for all sportsmen to realize that getting the best lenses for them is really a customized deal, since everyone is different," says Decot. "The best advice I can give is to consult a trained specialist to find out what works best for the individual sportsman."

Shooters who want more information on how eyes and shooting glasses work can contact Decot Hy-Wyd Sport Glasses, P.O. Box 15830, Phoenix, AZ 85060, or call 1-800-528-1901 for a free and very informative booklet.

HEARING PROTECTION

Did you hear the one about the three trap shooters who went fishing? The trio headed for a favorite fishing hole on a blustery day. They launched their boat, found a likely looking spot, tossed out bait, and began to wait.

"Boy, it sure is windy today," exclaimed the man in the bow as he held down his cap.

"You're wrong," shouted the man beside him. "It's Thursday!"

"Darn right I am!" screamed the third. "How about passing me a beer?"

It's a joke that holds both a good bit of humor and sad truth. For decades those who've shot a lot have paid a price with their hearing. And it isn't just trap and skeet shooters. The hundreds of days I've spent following dogs in the Kansas uplands have taken their toll on my ears. It's a little unsettling that I'm in my early thirties, and already I can't hear such high-pitched sounds as the flash charging on my camera. It's also frustrating when a father can't understand his three-year-old son because of background noise. Needless to say, I now wear ear protection just about any time I go shooting. This is especially true with sporting clays.

By the time sporting clays reached this country, most shooters were all too aware of the damage to hearing that shotgun noise could cause. Hearing protection has been the norm since the first courses were opened, and some courses even require shooters to protect their hearing.

Frankly, I can't imagine why anyone *wouldn't* want to wear hearing protectors. You see, while normal speech reaches about 60 decibels, the blast of a 12 gauge will usually score about 140 dB. Authorities say it only takes a noise of about 100 dB to cause physical discomfort, and continued exposure to noise from ninety to 100 dB can cause irreversible damage. Yes, giving your ears fifty doses of 140 dB in a single afternoon would be considered continued exposure. Even shooting a single round of sporting clays can irreversibly harm your ears.

Interestingly enough, the crash of a gun's recoil can do as much damage to your score as it can to your hearing. The noise of the gun is probably more to blame for your flinching than the recoil itself. Fear of the noise causes many shooters to tense up, and the anticipation of a pulled trigger and a painful ear can lead a shooter to shut his eyes and wince. It's impossible to shoot to your best ability under such conditions.

There are several kinds of good hearing protectors on the market. Prices range from what you'll pay for a pair of shotgun shells to the cost of an entire case of the same loads. What kind of hearing protector is the most effective? That's hard to measure. All help reduce the amount of noise that travels down the ear canal. Though none totally block the loud blast of a shotgun, most soften it down to bearable decibel readings.

The most common are simple earplugs. All reputable courses will have a jar or box filled with soft foam cylinders that easily fit into the ear. They're not the most comfortable hearing protector, but they are both functional and cheap. Many avid shooters buy them by the handful and carry plenty of spares in their shooting vest or bag. The plugs are usually disposed of at the day's end.

Rubber earplugs may also be used. These are very effective, though some shooters consider them to be too nonconforming and uncomfortable. They're very economical, as they generally cost only a few dollars and are reusable.

More and more shooters are turning to customized protectors that are actually molded to the ear canal. They fit much better than the rubber plugs and do a fine job of blocking damaging sound. Unfortunately, it's beginning to be a "buyer beware" market. A lot of people are cashing in on the craze and, to be blunt, there are a few who don't know what they're doing. In the past few months I've heard shooters complain about custom inserts that neither felt comfortable nor lasted long.

A good pair, however, is worth the $25 to $75 cost. Most major tournaments and sport shows will have a booth or two set up for the few-minute process. A number of my friends have spent the extra money and had their inserts made by a certified audiologist. All have been extremely pleased with the quality of the work and have recommended that I follow a similar course.

Last but not least are the traditional shooting muffs, which should cover the entire ear snugly. They work very well and aren't too expensive. Some shooters, however, feel that these interfere with gun mount, and others don't like the pressure on their heads. On the other hand, a

This shooter is both saving his hearing and guarding against flinching by wearing hearing protection. A variety of protectors are on the market. These inexpensive foam plugs will work well.

growing number of shooters are wearing the muffs with foam plugs for extra protection that makes sense and is very affordable.

There are a number of muffs on the market with small microphones that allow the shooter to hear normal noises such as voices. When the gun fires, the microphone is automatically shut off to protect the shooter's hearing.

There are enough kinds of hearing protectors on the market that there never has to be a situation like the one in the joke at the beginning of this chapter. But it's important that these devices be worn anytime we shoot, be it with a pistol at soda cans or a shotgun at doves. We also need to stress the importance of hearing protection for spectators. My children always wear hearing protection when they follow me on a hunt.

I hope that unlike me, when my son is grown, he won't have any difficulty understanding his child in a crowded mall or noisy car. I only hope I've checked the downslide in my own hearing in time so that I'll be able to get in on those same conversations with my grandson.

17

TRAPS

It all seems so simple and automatic that most of us take it for granted. We step into the station, position ourselves, and it all begins with the simple mutter of "pull." There's not enough time to think about the how and the why; once you see that disc zipping along faster than any grouse ever hoped to, it has your total concentration. No sooner have you patted yourself on the back for a great shot or made excuses for a poor one than you start the process over. Again, there's no thought to why that clay target gets to where it's going at such a darned fast speed.

Of course, there would be no sporting clays if it weren't for the targets and the traps. Most sporting clays traps, or throwers, are all but unique to the sport. The years since the sport first got started in Texas have seen a total revolution in American target throwers.

Unlike the regular trap and skeet target throwers, many sporting clays traps are set in natural surroundings. A good number are light enough to be carried and set up by one person. They also need to be cocked and loaded with a minimal amount of effort and in a scant few seconds. Some do it with human help, while others do it on their own. Yet these same throwers can launch a target for close to one hundred

A trapper throwing targets for shooters. The timbers and the big hay bale offer great protection.

yards at freeway speeds. They throw singles and doubles and a variety of targets.

Going into this book, I knew next to nothing about these amazing machines. I still know far less than some, but every little fact I learned gave me even more appreciation for the sport and its courses and stations. I hope the basic information that follows will give you an equal amount of admiration for traps and targets.

MANUAL-COCK, MANUAL-LOAD THROWERS

The most basic yet some of most impressive of all the target throwers are cocked and loaded by hand. The arm-cock type requires the trapper to grab the unit's arm and pull it 180 degrees back to the set position. The three-quarters-cocking thrower has the arm come about 75 percent of the way back to the loading position, while the half-cocking thrower forces the loader to pull the arm 180 degrees around to be cocked.

The lever-cock type uses a lever and sometimes a ratchet setup to get the arm around the thrower. With the added leverage, a heavier spring can be used on the trap for faster and farther-flying targets. These traps can also be cocked with less effort.

A cam-clutch below the arm on a manual or other thrower will freeze the unit's arm. The lack of vibration and flopping also allows for faster loading.

It usually takes only a matter of minutes to replace the regular single-target arm with one that will throw true pairs. With fewer moving parts, the manual throwers generally require the least amount of maintenance of all the traps. They're also easy to transport and have a relatively low price. As of this writing, some manual, arm-cock traps sell for as little as $300.

ELECTRIC-COCK, MANUAL-LOAD THROWERS
A little electricity can seemingly simplify things for a trap loader. Letting some juice pull the trap arm around to be cocked allows those of little strength to operate a unit. Properly set up, an electric-cocking unit will operate amazingly fast.

Several companies make throwers that operate off of standard twelve-volt batteries. Such units are very portable and can sometimes be hooked right up to a nearby vehicle. Those set up in the field will usually throw at least fifteen hundred targets before draining a battery. Still, the need to keep batteries charged and on hand can be somewhat of a hassle.

Others of these traps run off regular 110V/AC juice. One problem can be installing and wiring the proper electrical lines that such a machine requires. The need for a steady power supply makes such traps far less portable or versatile.

Though they basically throw an equal distance, electric-cock traps can be far more expensive than the simplest manual-cock thrower. Of the two types of electric cocks, the 110V/AC units are the more expensive. The presence of wires and circuits also makes electric-cock traps more of a maintenance problem. Still, most are well made enough to offer hundreds of hours of troublefree service.

Many course operators think the disadvantages are far outweighed by the advantages. Not only do electric-cock throwers allow almost anyone to use them, they're also safer since the trap operator doesn't have to cock the arm or lever.

ELECTRIC-COCK, AUTOMATIC-LOAD THROWERS
Traps that are loaded with stacks of targets then left to their electrical,

The most common targets in sporting clays from left to right—the mini, the midi, a standard and a battue. The bottom target is the popular rabbit target.

automatic selves are the cream of the crop. Since a "trapper" doesn't have to stay with the machine to load, overhead is decreased and the always-important safety factor is increased.

Such throwers can function with surprising quickness. Some models can rotate around, load, and fire in less than two seconds, meaning it's sometimes possible to have three or four targets in the air at the same time. But there are times when you have to pay for the ease of such miracle throwers. Autoloading throwers can turn sour, thanks to nothing more than a few bad targets. There are also remote areas and the supply of electricity to contend with.

Unlike manual-load throwers, the autoloaders basically throw only single, usually standard-size, targets. And though they save a lot on day-to-day overhead because they're unmanned, the do-it-all throwers can be quite pricey. Some sell for up to ten times what the most basic manual traps cost. Whether you get what you pay for depends on the setup, how much it's used, and how well the individual units perform.

An interesting type of electric, autoloading thrower is the oscillating thrower, which, as its name implies, stays on the move, never letting the shooter know the target's exact flight path. Some simply move from side to side, like those used in American trap, while others move both horizontally and vertically. These "wobble traps" add the ultimate in realism to a hunting situation. The privilege of such shooting doesn't come cheaply, however. One such thrower often costs more than all of the traps combined on some local courses.

Like most throwers, the oscillating traps can be triggered remotely by electrical switch or by voice. Some courses feature an arrangement whereby a shooter deposits a token and gets a certain number of targets. It's a great way to practice up on a particular station.

18

TARGETS

Shotgun targets have a much more colorful history than most of us realize. Shortly after breech-loading shotguns came to popularity following the Civil War, shooters devised a setup that made things surprisingly realistic. The targets were usually glass balls stuffed with feathers or dry leaves. When the target was hit, a cloud of feathers or leaves would gently float to the ground. Tossed into the air by a variety of catapults and throwers, the heavy targets were slow and easy to hit, even with the black-powder guns.

Today's sporting clays targets are anything but slow or consistently easy to hit. No doubt the variety of targets offered adds to the specialness of sporting clays.

STANDARDS

There's a little bit of deviation between what's considered a standard-sized target in the U.S. and in Europe. Here in the States we've been sniping at targets that are roughly 108 millimeters for decades. Across the Atlantic the standard target is a touch larger, at about 110 millimeters.

By far the most common targets on sporting clays courses, standard

The fully automatic thrower is the cream of the crop. Though some cost in excess of $10,000, this set-up by Hunters Pointe is affordable enough that an individual can purchase a machine and throw his own targets.

targets come in an assortment of colors. From time to time a course will throw in an off-colored target to add further realism to a pheasant or duck station. For instance, if most of the targets are orange, an occasional white target will be tossed to simulate a hen bird flying in front of the gun. A shooter who breaks such a target is usually penalized in some form.

Standards are by far the most affordable targets, only costing about half as much as the specialty targets. They're also fairly easy to break. Most experienced shooters pick the pellet size depending on the range. Any skeet shooter will testify that number 9 shot will smoke a standard-size target at reasonably close range.

MIDIS
The next size down is a 90-millimeter target called a midi. For those who aren't up on metric measurements, the midi is just the right size to

fit inside a standard target. In fact, some courses will slide a midi inside a standard target for a fun double off a single-arm thrower.

Normally all black or orange, these medium-size targets are often used to simulate the flight of such birds as ruffed and prairie grouses. Midis also do a great job of duplicating the birds' great speed, as they're just the right size to fly fast and far. They're generally as easy to break as a standard, if you can hit them; most shooters prefer number 8 shot to assure a good density.

As with all of the specialty targets, midis are fairly expensive. Perhaps the sport's growth will increase the demand for midis and bring production costs down so that more courses will be able to use them.

MINIS

The runt of sporting clays targets, a mini is 60 millimeters, about the size of a snuff can. Shooting minis would be the bird-hunting equivalent of firing at hummingbirds, though the targets are usually thrown to simulate doves or snipes.

The small size of minis makes them quick out of a trap, but their lack of weight causes them to slow rather quickly. Judging speed can be a problem, as can figuring distance. After looking at standard-size targets for years, a shooter may simply have a problem spotting minis. This problem can be compounded by a screening of tree branches. A lot of shooters feel intimidated by the small targets because they see so few of them.

A mini is actually fairly easy to break—once you get your pattern around it. A single pellet will often do the job. But because of the target's small size, many shooters opt for number 9 shot to ensure a good, dense pattern.

BATTUES

No one I've talked to seems to know the exact meaning of the word "battue." Having shot at them, I figure it's some foreign term for *&%$! These "flying pancakes" are a little wider than a standard American target, but only about one-quarter inch thick.

The thin targets fly fast but don't settle to the earth gently like most targets. Instead they tend to turn on edge and drop quickly. Some shooters try to hit them while they're falling because there's more

This shooter is trying to break a mini way over the pines. The different sized targets add extra fun to the game.

surface to shoot at. A battue that's flying strong and true doesn't give a shooter much to hit. Most shooters rely on 7½s or stout 8s to break these often-frustrating targets.

RABBITS
The bouncing and running rabbit target can be easy to hit if you can time the shot with a high bounce. For this stoutest of all targets on a range, a load of 7½s will do the trick well.

ROCKETS
Similar to battues in size but thicker, rockets are usually launched vertically into the air. These fast-flying targets, which are sometimes used to simulate springing teal, can be tough to hit and to break. Choke will vary depending on range, but 7½s are the norm. Rockets are very expensive, as are battues, and they're usually only shot on the best courses.

19

SAFETY

Despite the antigun hysteria that's sweeping our nation, shotguns and the shooting sports, including sporting clays, are safe. The untarnished safety image of sporting clays hasn't come about by accident—it's come from the forethought and diligence of course designers and owners, station attendants, trap loaders, and most important, the average shooter.

But all it's going to take is one accident—one discharge that hits a spectator, one flaw in the many protections of a trap operator—and we'll all lose. News of an accidental shooting death at a sporting clays course would no doubt be jumped on by the media. The antigun movement would surely use such a tragedy to its advantage, possibly leading some people who've been riding the fence to join the cause.

Local and state laws governing such events might then be tightened, and no doubt insurance rates would jump significantly. But worst of all, there would be the pain and suffering of the victim and his or her family and the troubled consciences of those who were present and responsible. If we all do our parts, however, that accident may never come to pass.

Sporting clays has several rules that make safety come as second

This is a prime example of a simple shooting station that helps add the maximum safety to a course. The sides keep the shooter from shooting toward the trap, and the bar on top keeps the gun from being raised too far overhead.

nature for shooters. For example, you may not load a gun until you're within a station, with the gun's muzzle pointed safely away from the station and spectators. The following is a complete list of rules for USSCA-sanctioned shoots.

USSCA SAFETY REQUIREMENTS

1. Ear protection—noise damage is permanent and not reversible, and well documented as caused by shooting noise. Either the ear muff or the molded insert type are acceptable. Some individuals use both. Not required but highly recommended.

2. Eye protection—with semiautomatic shotguns the possibility of a blow-back must be guarded against, and shooting incoming targets will cause some pieces of targets to fall on the shooter. Shooting glasses should be worn at all times. Not required but recommended.

3. Gun action—must remain open at all times, with no shells in chamber or magazine. Failure to follow this safety procedure

will result in one warning by the Field Judge. Subsequent violations may result in disqualification without return of entry fees.

4. Gun may be loaded and action closed only when in position to shoot in the designated shooting station. Failure to follow this safety procedure will result in one warning by the Field Judge. Subsequent violations may result in disqualification without return of entry fees.

5. Use no shot larger in size than 7½ lead. [Larger shot carries farther and retains its damaging energy longer.] Number 8 and 9 shot are legal. Failure to follow this safety procedure will result in one warning by the Field Judge. Subsequent violations may result in disqualification without return of entry fees.

6. Before shooting from a station, always be certain that adjacent fields within your range of fire (up to 300 yards) are clear of other shooters and spectators. Failure to follow this safety procedure will result in one warning by the Field Judge. Subsequent violations may result in disqualification without return of entry fees.

7. While waiting your turn to shoot, be certain that your position does not infringe upon the shooter's line of fire or field of view.

We cannot, however, just relax and rely on the established rules and the precautions of course personnel. Every shooter must think and preach safety. If you see a breach of the safety rules, make the person aware of the problem. If you notice a chink in the armor of a course, the owner will welcome your observations and ideas.

Sporting clays will continue to be as safe a sport as it is fun if we all work together.

List of Sporting Clays Courses

Some of the clubs in this listing are in the developmental stages, and others are private and are only open to the public on a limited basis. Be sure to call to find out days and hours of operation.

ARIZONA
Sanders LaGrue Hunt Club
Humphrey, AZ (501) 673-2796
Arizona Hunt Club
Shooting Sports
Mayer, AZ (602) 632-7709

ARKANSAS
Sugar Creek Sporting Clays
Bentonville, AR (501) 273-0848
Nevada Gamebirds
Buckner, AR (501) 899-2902
Grandview Plantation
Sports Club
Columbus, AR (501) 983-2526
Crowley Ridge Shooting Resort
Forrest City, AR (501) 633-3352
L'anguille River Hunt Club
Forrest City, AR (501) 633-8195

CALIFORNIA
Birds Landing Hunting
Preserve
Birds Landing, CA (707) 374-5092
River Road Sporting Clays
Gonzales, CA (408) 675-2473
Antelope Valley Sportsmen's
Club
Lancaster, CA (805) 724-1291
Ozena Valley Sportsman's Club
Maricopa, CA (805) 766-2522
Pachmayr Hunt School
Monrovia, CA (818) 357-7771
Raahauge's Shotgun Sports
Norco, CA (714) 735-2361
Sacramento Sporting Clays
Pleasant Grove, CA
(916) 656-2544

Moore-N-Moore Sporting Clays
San Fernando, CA (818) 890-4788

Winchester Canyon Gun Club
Santa Barbara, CA (805) 965-9890

COLORADO
Bang-Away Gun Club
Berthoud, CO (303) 535-4538

Mt. Blanca Game Bird & Trout
Blanca, CO (719) 379-1681

Broadmoor Shooting Grounds
Colorado Springs, CO
(719) 635-3438

Rocky Mountain Roosters
Colorado Springs, CO
(719) 635-3257

High Country Game Birds
Elizabeth, CO (303) 646-3315

Glenarm Sporting Clays
Glenwood Springs, CO
(303) 249-6490

CONNECTICUT
Bristol Game & Fish
Association
Bristol, CT (203) 879-9938

Madison Rod & Gun Club
Madison, CT (203) 245-3515

Connecticut Travelers
Sporting Clays
New Milford, CT (203) 354-9351

DELAWARE
Ommelanden Shooting
Grounds
New Castle, DE (302) 328-2256

FLORIDA
Sandestin
Destin, FL (904) 267-8111

Big D Sporting Clays
Lake City, FL (904) 752-0594

Tampa Sporting Clays
Odessa, FL (813) 986-7770

Orange County Trap & Skeet
Orlando, FL (407) 351-1230

Rocky Comfort Hunting
Preserve
Quincy, FL (904) 627-8074

Indian River Trap & Skeet Club
Vero Beach, FL (407) 231-1783

GEORGIA
Heartbreak Ridge
Sporting Clays
Albany, GA (912) 439-8081

Hunt Close Plantation
Atlanta, GA (404) 980-0606

Pinetucky Skeet & Trap Club
Augusta, GA (404) 738-0204

Pigeon Mountain
Sporting Clays
Chickamauga, GA (404) 398-3420

Cherokee Rose Plantation
Griffin, GA (404) 228-CLAY

Southern Wings Plantation
Harrison, GA (800) 272-1617

The Meadows National
Gun Club
Smarr, GA (912) 994-9910

Bear Sports Center
Thomasville, GA (912) 228-0209

Myrtlewood Plantation
Thomasville, GA (912) 226-0611

HAWAII
Schofield Rod & Gun Club
Honolulu, HI (808) 955-0771

IDAHO
Buz Fawcett's Shooting Grounds
Meridian, ID (208) 888-3415

ILLINOIS
Seneca Hunt Club
Maywood, IL (312) 681-2582

Midwest Shooting Sports
Thompsonville, IL (618) 982-2906

Diamond S Sporting Clays
Tremont, IL (309) 449-5500

Trout & Grouse
Shooting Grounds
Wilmette, IL (312) 251-8090

INDIANA
West Creek Hunting Preserve
Cedar Lake, IN (219) 696-6101

Shotgun Hollow
Cloverdale, IN (317) 653-4586

Tippecanoe Sporting Clays
W. Lafayette, IN (317) 743-1809

IOWA
Triple H Game Preserve &
Sporting Clays
Burlington, IA (319) 985-2253

Blackhawk Sporting Clays
Cedar Falls, IA (319) 987-2625

Outpost Clays Range &
Hunting Preserve
Logan, IA (712) 644-2222

Southern Iowa Sporting Clays
Moulton, IA (515) 642-3256

Lazy H Hunting Club
Woodbine, IA (712) 647-2877

KANSAS
Cedar Hill Gun Club &
Sporting Clays
Baldwin, KS (913) 843-8213

Flint Oak Ranch
Fall River, KS (316) 658-4401

Marals Des Cygnes
Sporting Park
Ottawa, KS (913) 242-SHOT

Ravenwood Hunting Preserve
Topeka, KS (913) 256-6444

KENTUCKY
Shoot-Fire
Bowling Green, KY (502) 781-9545

LOUISIANA
High Point Shooting Grounds
Belle Chasse, LA (504) 656-7575

Wild Wings Sporting Clays
Downsville, LA (318) 982-7777

MAINE
Foggy Ridge Game Bird Farm
Warren, ME (207) 273-2357

MARYLAND
MNCPPC/Prince George
Shooting Center
Glenn Dale, MD (301) 577-7177

Fairfield Shooting Sports
Henderson, MD (301) 750-1824

Hopkins Game Farm
Kennedyville, MD (301) 348-5287

I & P Hunting Lodge
Sudlersville, MD (301) 438-3832

MASSACHUSETTS
Walpole Sportsmen's Association
Walpole, MA (617) 545-4725

Falmouth Skeet Club
Waquoit, MA (508) 540-3177

MICHIGAN
Bay County Conservation &
Gun Club
Farwell, MI (517) 631-9944

Grand Blanc Huntsman Club
Grand Blanc, MI (313) 636-7261

Boyne Sporting Clays Club
Harbour Springs, MI (616)
537-4830

Hunters Ridge Hunt Club
Oxford, MI (313) 628-4868

MINNESOTA
Wild Marsh Sports Shoot
Association
Clearlake, MN (612) 662-2292

Crookston Gun Club
Crookston, MN (218) 281-5143

Le Blanc's Rice Creek Hunting
Little Falls, MN (612) 745-2451

Royal Flush Shooting Club
Little Falls, MN (612) 745-2522

Minnesota Horse & Hunt Club
Prior Lake, MN (612) 447-2272

Clear Creek Shooting Preserve
Wrenshall, MN (218) 384-3670

MISSISSIPPI
Quailwood Plantation
Holly Springs, MS (601) 357-2660

Wilderness West
Jackson, MS (601) 956-4762

**Whistling Wings Country
Sporting Clays**
Lucedale, MS (601) 947-8964

MISSOURI
Trail Ridge Outdoor Adventures
Blairstown, MO (816) 885-3632

Ozark Shooters Sports Complex
Branson, MO (417) 820-3766

United Sportsmen's Club
Jefferson City, MO (314) 882-3562

**Wildwood Hunting &
Sporting Clays**
Houstonia, MO (816) 879-4451

Kansas City Shooting School
Kansas City, MO (816) 734-4044

**Pond Fort Kennels &
Hunt Club**
O'Fallon, MO (314) 327-5680

**Black Hawk Valley Hunting
Preserve**
Old Monroe, MO (314) 665-5459

Game Hill Hunting Club
Weston, MO (816) 431-5057

MONTANA
Sport Montana
Billings, MT (406) 252-8188

Perry Hunt & Adventures
Fort Benton, MT (406) 622-5336

Royal Bighorn Lodge
St. Xavier, MT (406) 666-2340

NEBRASKA
Grand Island Sporting Clays
Grand Island, NE (402) 463-8580

NEVADA
**Peppermill's Arvada Ranch
Gun Club**
Mesquite, NV (800) 621-0187

Topaz Sportsmen's Center
Wellington, NV (702) 266-3512

Flying M Hunting Club
Yerington, NV (702) 463-5260

NEW HAMPSHIRE
SKAT Shooting Preserve
New Ipswich, NH (603) 878-1257

Dexter Sporting Clays
West Lebanon, NH (603) 448-5552

NEW JERSEY
West Creek Sporting Clays
Eldora, NJ (609) 861-2760

**Oldman's Creek Farm &
Sporting Club**
Pedricktown, NJ (215) 647-7973

Buckshorn Sportsmen Club
Salem, NJ (609) 935-4659

Fox Ridge Range
Sussex, NJ (201) 875-5791

NEW MEXICO
**Circle Diamond Ranch
Sporting Clays**
Tinnie, NM (505) 653-4957

NEW YORK
Goose Creek Hunt Club
Ashville, NY (716) 782-2529

**Hendrick Hudson Fish &
Game Club**
Averill Park, NY (518) 674-5184

Cedar Hill Shooting Preserve
Germantown, NY (518) 828-9360

Advertising Sportsmen of
New York
Holmes, NY (212) 947-5151

Peconic Sportsmen's Club
Manorville, NY (516) 727-5248

Whaleback Farms
Shooting Preserve
Middlesex, NY (716) 381-7250

Sandanona Sporting Clays
Millbrook, NY (914) 677-9701

Mid-Hudson Trap & Skeet
New Paltz, NY (914) 255-7460

Dutchess Valley Rod &
Gun Club
Pawling, NY (914) 855-5014

Pawling Mountain Club
Pawling, NY (914) 855-3825

Mashomack Fish &
Game Preserve
Pine Plains, NY (212) 249-4638

Rochester-Brooks Gun Club
Rush, NY (716) 533-9913

Morris Creek Fish &
Game Preserve
South New Berlin, NY (607)
263-5238

NORTH CAROLINA
Beaver Dam Sporting
Clays Range
Greenville, NC (919) 758-2266

Adams Creek Sporting Clays
Havelock, NC (919) 447-7688

Deep River Sporting Clays
Raleigh, NC (919) 774-7080

Dove Roost Sporting Clays
Shawboro, NC (919) 232-3188

OHIO
Ruff Shot Sporting Clays
Carrollton, OH (216) 343-0363

W.R. Hunt Club
Clyde, OH (419) 547-8550

Hill-N-Dale
Medina, OH (216) 725-2097

OKLAHOMA
Southern Ranch Lodge &
Hunting Club
Chandler, OK (405) 258-0000

Thunderbird Sporting Clays
Vici, OK (405) 995-4220

OREGON
Briarwood Sporting Clays
Eugene, OR (503) 344-7224

T.R.E.O. Corporation
Heppner, OR (503) 676-5840

PENNSYLVANIA
Hillside Hunting Preserve
Berlin, PA (814) 267-4484

Gap-View Sporting Clays
Dalmatia, PA (717) 761-7779

Hunting Hills
Dilliner, PA (412) 324-2142

Rough Cut Sporting Clays
Edinboro, PA (814) 734-1595

Chestnut Ridge Sporting Clays
Latrobe, PA (412) 539-2070

Oakmont Country Club
Oakmont, PA (412) 683-7396

Laurel Hill Hunting Preserve
Rockwood, PA (814) 352-7063

T.N.T. Hunting Preserve
Smock, PA (412) 677-2609

Busted Flush
Titusville, PA (814) 827-4030

RHODE ISLAND
Quack Sporting Clays
Cumberland, RI (401) 723-8202

Addieville East Farm
Mapleville, RI (401) 568-3185

SOUTH CAROLINA
Brays Island Plantation
Beaufort, SC (803) 525-6303

Boykin Mill Sporting Clays
Camden, SC (803) 432-4332

Charleston Sporting Clays
Charleston, SC (803) 884-6194

The Oaks Gun Club
Georgetown, SC (803) 527-1861

River Bend Sportsman's Resort
Inman, SC (803) 592-1348

SOUTH DAKOTA
Dakota Sharpshooter
SKAT Courses
Madison, SD (605) 256-3636

Valley West Trap & Sporting Clays
Sioux Falls, SD (605) 361-3173

TENNESSEE
Dunaway Hunting & Fishing Club
Chattanooga, TN (615) 756-4860

Grinders Switch Farm
Nashville, TN (615) 373-8340

TEXAS
Sporting Clays Int. of Dallas
Allen, TX (214) 727-1998

Cypress Valley Preserve
Austin, TX (512) 825-3396

One In One Hundred Gun Club
Beaumont, TX (409) 755-9903

Joshua Creek Ranch
Boerne, TX (612) 537-9136

Re-Bob Enterprises
Breckenridge, TX (817) 559-9578

La Paloma Sporting Club
Bulverde, TX (512) 438-4424

Upland Bird Country
Corsicana, TX (903) 872-5663

Three Amigos Sporting Clays
El Campo, TX (409) 543-1109

Circle Bar Sporting Clays
Fluvanna, TX (915) 573-7469

Alpine Range
Ft. Worth, TX (817) 478-6613

TargetMaster Sportsmen's Club
Garland, TX (903) 343-4545

Kat Creek Sporting Clays
Henderson, TX (903) 854-2232

Honey Creek Sporting Clays
Hico, TX (817) 796-2148

American Shooting Centers
Houston, TX (713) 556-1597

Champion Lake Gun Club
Houston, TX (713) 893-5868

Clear Creek Gun Range
League City, TX (713) 337-1722

Dallas Gun Club
Lewisville, TX (214) 462-0043

Rustic Range Sporting Clays
Lubbock, TX (806) 828-4820

Greene Creek Sporting Clays
Stephenville, TX (817) 965-9250

Utopia On The River
Utopia, TX (512) 966-2444

Tierra Colinas
Weatherford, TX (817) 594-5001

UTAH
Porcupine Adventures
Sporting Clays
Paradise, UT (801) 245-4555

VERMONT
Hermitage Shooting Grounds
Wilmington, VT (802) 464-3759

VIRGINIA
Eastern Shore Sporting Clays
Jamesville, VA (804) 442-7684

WEST VIRGINIA
Fayette Shooting Sports
Hazelton, WV (412) 437-4200

Foxy Pheasant
Hunting Preserve
Kearneysville, WV (304) 725-4963

WISCONSIN
Trout & Grouse
Shooting Grounds
Kenosha, WI (414) 857-7232

River Wildlife
Kohler, WI (414) 457-0134

Top Gun Sporting Clays
Woodland, WI (414) 349-3108

WYOMING
Pheasant Meadows Gun Club
Douglas, WY (307) 358-5212

CANADA
Spring Lake Country Club
Sundre, Alberta (403) 638-2040

Club Roue du Roy
Hemmingford, Quebec
(514) 247-2882

Montreal Skeet Club
PT-Viau, Laval, Quebec
(514) 452-2417

DOMINICAN REPUBLIC
Casa de Campo
Dominican Republic
(809) 523-3333

OFFICIAL RULES AND REGULATIONS NATIONAL SPORTING CLAYS ASSOCIATION

ORGANIZATION OF THE NATIONAL SPORTING CLAYS ASSOCIATION

The National Sporting Clays Association, a Division of the National Skeet Shooting Association, was formed in April 1989 to promote sporting clays in the United States and Canada.

The National Sporting Clays Association (NSCA) is a nonprofit organization owned and operated by and for its members. The primary objective of the NSCA is to promote the growth of sporting clays in a way which is beneficial to all who enjoy and participate in the game. The division of NSCA, is guided by an Advisory Council comprised of range owners, both competitive and recreational shooters and the shooting industry.

The following is an informative summary of the organization of the National Sporting Clays Association. The Official National Sporting Clays Rules govern the shooting of registered targets, the conduct of shooters and the duties of shoot management. The NSCA has the responsibility for the formulation, regulation and enforcement of these rules. These rules are contained in this booklet.

The NSCA reserves the right to make alteration in, or amendments to these rules at any time, whenever it deems it to be in the best interest of the National Sporting Clays Association.

GENERAL INFORMATION

A. PURPOSE OF NSCA
The purpose of the National Sporting Clays Association is to promote and govern the sport of sporting clays throughout the United States and Canada. The NSCA is dedicated to the development of the sport at all levels of participation. We vow to create an atmosphere of healthy competition and meaningful fellowship within its membership. We also offer the hunter a recreational target shooting game, which will strengthen his hunting and gun safety skills and extend his shooting season.

B. MEMBERSHIP
Annual membership dues are $30.00 a year with a copy of the official monthly magazine, Sporting Clays, "The Shotgun Hunters' Magazine". A $20.00 membership is available to dependents (no magazine).

The membership and shooting year is from January 1 to December 31.

Application for annual membership may be made at any registered shoot by filling out an application or by contacting the NSCA for an application.

C. CLASSIFICATION
1. LEWIS CLASS
After reviewing all forms of classification, the Advisory Council recommended the Lewis Class System for classification, mostly because of the wide variations of difficulty level for range layouts. This system is based on the final scores as they are posted when the shoot has been completed and gives every contestant an equal chance to win, no matter what his shooting ability.

Until we have a fair tract record on course layout, this system is highly recommended. This does not mean we are forcing you to use this system, but only the recommendation of the Council. See below for Lewis Class System.

2. BLIND DRAW
In using this system, management decides which fields to be used. Generally, this system uses half the fields shot during the event and the total score from those fields are added together and multiplied by two (2). This figure is then used on a classification table to determine the shooter's class for that days shooting.

3. STENCIL SYSTEM
This system also takes into account half the targets shot during the event. Several basic rules apply to this system such as:

a. Cut out 50% of the shots per field but never use the first two shots.

b. Shoot management should not disclose this stencil to any participants.

c. As shooters finish, take the overlay stencil and place it on the card and add all (hit) targets and multiply by two (2).

This will give you the average which can be used with the classification schedule to assign a class for each shooter.

4. The "average method" is yet another way of classifying and the following rules apply:

A new shooter will attain his classification after shooting 300 targets. He will reclassify after each 300 targets, 600 targets, 900 targets, etc.

Shooters must always reclassify at the end of each regular string (300 targets) even though the correct number of targets for reclassification comes between the preliminary and the main event. Reclassification is not effective until AFTER the shoot, but must be accomplished on the correct number of targets.

During the current year, a shooter is subject to reclassify UPWARD ONLY.

Reclassification DOWN will only be accomplished by NSCA at the beginning of the next sporting clays year. However, you may only go down ONE CLASS.

CLASS	AVERAGES
AA	75 & Above
A	65–74.99
B	55–64.99
C	54.99 & Below

D. RULES OF CONDUCT OF NSCA SHOOTER

Each member will be furnished a copy of these Official NSCA rules, with the understanding that the member will read and understand each rule. Members are strongly encouraged to know these rules and abide by them, both for their own benefit and for the benefit of other shooters.

By entering the competition, every person agrees to accept all official decisions and to abide by these rules.

When making your entry at any registered shoot, produce your plastic identification card and your average card so that your name, address and membership number are properly noted and errors in records prevented. Shooters not having his/her plastic card should always list their NSCA number, entire name and address on the event cards.

The score card is intended for the purpose of providing the classification committees at the shoots with up to date data on your shooting ability. Shooters not having their cards up to date may be put in a higher class or otherwise penalized.

It is the duty of each NSCA member to have his/her average card updated at the end of each shoot.

Failure to accurately record scores, or the falsification of scores, can lead to suspension from the NSCA.

E. CONCURRENT EVENTS

Concurrent events will be offered in:
Lady—Junior—Senior
Junior—any person who has not reached his 18th birthday.
Senior—any person who has reached his 60th birthday.

The Advisory Council is considering the possibility of adding other concurrent events. Pending results shoot management may offer other concurrent categories; such as, Sub-Junior, Sub-Senior, Sub-Sub-Senior and Veteran.

F. TOURNAMENTS
Only clubs affiliated with NSCA shall be eligible to conduct registered shoots.

Only members in good standing who have paid their annual dues may participate in a registered NSCA shoots.

RULES AND REGULATIONS
I. DEFINITION OF TERMS

A. SHOOT PROMOTER
Individual(s) or entity which provides for the facilities and organization of the competition. Shoot Promoters may also act as Shoot Officials.

B. SHOOT OFFICIALS
Individual(s) appointed by the Shoot Promoter and responsible for course layout, target selection, and appointment of Field Judges. Shoot Officials shall be responsible for both layout and testing of the course. Shoot Officials are responsible for ensuring that competitors are not allowed to test or preview the course prior to the competition.

C. FIELD JUDGE
Person over 18 years of age assigned by the Shoot Officials to score targets and enforce the rules.

D. STATION
A shooting position from which one or more targets are attempted.

E. FIELD
A station or group of stations from which targets are attempted sequentially. Once a squad or individual checks into a "field", all "stations" and/or all targets on the "field" are attempted before moving to another "field". The Shoot Officials will provide direction for execution of shooting at each field.

F. REPORT PAIR
Two sequential targets where the second target is launched at the sound of the gun firing at the first target.

G. FOLLOWING PAIR
Two sequential targets where the second target is launched at the officials discretion after the first target.

H. SIMULTANEOUS PAIR
Two targets launched simultaneously.

II. EQUIPMENT

A. TARGETS
Targets thrown in any event may include any or all of the following:

1. Regulation SKEET or TRAP targets as specified by ATA, NSSA or ISU.

2. Mini, midi, battue rocket, or rabbit targets as specified by FITASC.

3. Propeller mounted ZZ-Pigeon targets.

4. Any sporting clays target approved by Shoot Officials.

5. "Poison Bird" targets of a separate and clearly discernable appearance may be included at random. Shooters attempting shots at these targets shall be scored a "miss" or "lost bird". Shooters correctly refraining from attempting the "poison bird" (protected species) will be scored as a "hit" or "dead bird".

6. Target number and selection for any competition shall be at the discretion of the Shoot Officials. No more than 30% of the total number of targets shall be other than targets described in A-1. Target number and selection shall be the same for all shooters.

B. SHOTGUNS
1. Shotguns of 12 gauge or smaller gauges, in safe working order, and capable of firing two shots are to be used in attempting all targets.

2. Shotguns fitted for multiple barrels (of various chokes and/or lengths) are permitted. The shooter is allowed to change barrels only between stations or as otherwise directed by the Shoot Officials.

3. Shotguns with interchangeable or adjustable chokes are permitted at the shooter's discretion. Chokes can be changed only between stations or as otherwise directed by the Shoot Officials.

4. Competitors may enter a shoot with various guns and attempt targets at various stations with different guns, or the gun of another competitor. Guns may be changed only between stations or as otherwise directed by the Shoot Officials.

C. AMMUNITION
1. All shot shell ammunition including reloads may be used. Shoot Officials may further limit the ammunition to be commercially manufactured.

2. Loads for 12 gauge guns shall not exceed $1^1/8$ ounces of shot charge.

3. Maximum shot charge for any given competition may be further limited by the Shoot Officials.

4. Shot size shall not exceed U.S. #$7^1/2$ (diameter 0.095"; wt. 1.07 grains).

5. Shot shall be normal production spherical shot. Plated shot is permitted.

D. THE COURSE

1. The course will provide for a predetermined number of shooting fields from which each competitor will attempt various targets. The number of "Stations" and the number and characteristics of targets from each station, on each field, will be determined by the Shoot Officials, and will be the same for all shooters.

2. Targets will be propelled by, and launched from, any of a number of commercially produced, modified, or handmade devices which will propel an approved target in a manner to approach the characteristics (in the opinion of the Shoot Officials) of a game bird or animal typically taken by a sporting shotgun.

3. Launching devices which provide for targets traveling at varying angles and distances to the competitors are acceptable (i.e. wobble traps). No more than 20% of the targets shall be presented from such devices. No less than 80% of all targets in a shoot shall be presented with a reasonably consistent trajectory, distance and velocity to all shooters.

4. Devices which provide for propelling multiple targets are permitted.

5. Devices propelling targets of more than one type, and devices capable of providing targets at varying angles and distances, shall be employed only as the varying aspects of these devices will be the same for all shooters and will be free of all human element of selection.

6. Field Judges will be required at each station in sufficient number to competently enforce all "rules for the shooter", as well as, to score the attempts accurately. Numbers and positions for Field Judges shall be determined by the Shoot Officials.

III. EXECUTION OF THE SHOOT

A. SHOOTING ORDER

Contestants shall proceed through the course and competition in one of the following formats:

1. European Rotation

Individual competitors or groups of 2 through 5 competitors will proceed to the various stations. Groups may shoot in any order selected by the shooters. The squad or group shooting the stations of any field may be changed from field to field.

2. Squading

At the discretion of the shoot officials, groups of 3 to 5 shooters will be formed to proceed from field to field in a fixed sequence.

3. In European Rotation, a shoot start and shoot end time will be established. It will be the responsibility of each shooter to complete the entire event between these times.

4. In squading sequence, squads will be assigned a start time and it is the responsibility of each shooter to be ready on time, or within no more than 5 minutes of that time.

5. In either case, shots not attempted by the "shoot end time" (European Rotation), or shots not attempted by the shooter joining his squad after they have begun (squading), those targets not attempted will be scored as "lost". The Shoot Officials shall have the right to provide for make up targets if sufficient justification can be presented. Make up targets are provided solely at the discretion of the Shoot officials.

6. Rotation of Order
In squads of shooters, rotation of shooting order is permitted between stations. Rotation may be formatted by Shoot Officials, to be followed by all squads. If not prescribed by Shoot Officials, order will be determined by shooters.

7. Shooters Viewing Targets
There will be no "view targets" for any shooter on station. In the instance of the commencement of shooting, or if no station has had a contestant on the line for 15 minutes or longer, targets may be presented for viewing from locations normally accessible to spectators.

B. ATTEMPTING TARGETS
Targets will be presented for attempt at each station in one or more of the following formats.

1. Single Target/Single Shot

2. Single Target/Two Shots
The target will be scored "hit" or "dead" if successfully attempted on either shot.

3. Doubles/Two Shots
Doubles may be presented as report, following, or simultaneous pairs. In simultaneous pairs the shooter has the right to shoot either of the targets first. If the shooter has missed the first target he may fire the second cartridge at the same target.

When shooting report or following pairs, the shooter will have the right if missing the first target to fire the second cartridge at the same target (the result being scored on the first target and the second target being scored as lost).

Should the shooter break both targets with either the first or the second shot then the result will be scored as two "kills".

4. Multiple Target/Two Shots
Two hits or dead birds maximum.

5. Stations at which the shooter is walking are permitted. (See Section VIII-C)

6. Time Reloads
Targets presented with set time periods for shooter to reload prior to the presentation of the subsequent targets are permitted. Five Seconds is the normal reload time but other intervals may be used at the discretion of the Shoot Official(s).

IV. RULES FOR THE SHOOTER

A. LOW GUN
Gun stock must be visible below the shooters armpit.

B. CALL FOR TARGET
Target will be launched immediately or with a delay of up to 3 seconds.

C. MOUNTING OF GUN
Shooter is to keep from mounting his gun until target is visible. If in the judgment of the Field Judge, the shooter moves to mount his gun prior to seeing the target, the target will be a "no bird" and the sequence and call will begin again. No penalty will be assessed the shooter. Excessive "no bird" (3 per day) can be construed as cause for scoring targets as lost.

D. SHOOTER'S RESPONSIBILITY
It will be the responsibility of each shooter to be familiar with these rules. Ignorance of the rules will not be a cause to "re-attempt" targets lost because of rule violations.

V. SCORING

A. Targets shall be scored as "hit" or "killed" or "dead" and designated on score cards by an (X) when in the opinion of the Field Judge, a visible piece has been broken from the target. Targets not struck and broken by the shooters shot shall be called "lost" or "missed" and designated on score cards by a (O).

B. The call of "lost" or "dead", "hit" or "miss" shall be announced by the Field Judge prior to recording the score on every target.

C. If the shooter disagrees with the Field Judge's call, he must protest before firing at another set of targets or before leaving that station. The Field Judge may poll the spectators and may reverse his original call. In all cases the final decision of the Field Judge will stand.

D. Each shooter will be assigned a score card to be presented to the Field Judges at the various stations or fields. Field Judges will score each shooter's attempts on the individual's score card. The total shall be tallied and the scores written in ink and initiated by the Field Judge.

E. Each shooter is responsible for his score card from assignment, at the start of the shoot, until the card is filed with the Shoot Officials at the end of each day's shooting.

F. Shooters are responsible for checking the Field Judge's totals of "hits and misses" at each station and/or field.

VI. MALFUNCTIONS

A. The shooter shall be allowed a combined total of two malfunctions per day attributed to either the shooters gun or ammo. Targets not attempted due to the third or latter malfunction shall be scored as "lost". Targets not attempted on the two allowed malfunctions shall be treated as "no birds".

1. GUN MALFUNCTIONS

    a. In the case of a gun malfunction, the shooter must remain in place, the gun pointed safely down range and must not open the gun or tamper with trigger, safety or barrel selector, until the field judge has determined the cause and made his ruling.

    b. Targets shall be scored as lost if the shooter is unable to fire because of the following. Examples include but are not limited to:

        1. Shooter has left the safety on.
        2. Shooter has forgotten to load or properly cock the gun.
        3. Shooter has forgotten to disengage the locking device from the magazine of an automatic weapon.
        4. Shooter has not sufficiently released the trigger of a single trigger gun having fired the first shot.

    c. If the shooter fails to comply with item VI-A-1-a, the target or targets will be scored as lost or missed.

2. AMMO MALFUNCTIONS

    a. In the case of an ammunition malfunction, the shooter must remain in place, the gun pointing safely down range and must not open the gun or tamper with the trigger, safety or barrel selector, until the field judge has determined the cause and made his ruling.

    b. Examples include, but are not limited to:

        1. Failure to fire, provide firing pin indentation is clearly noticeable.
        2. One in which the primer fires, but through failure of the shell or lack of components, and which, consequently leaves part of or all of the charge of shot or wad in the gun. A soft load, in which the shot and wad leave the barrel, is not a misfire.
        3. Brass pulling off hull between shots on doubles.
        4. Separation of brass from casing when gun is fired (usually accompanied by a "whistling" sound as the plastic sleeve leaves the barrel).

    c. If the shooter fails to comply with item VI-A-2-a, the target or targets will be scored as "lost" or "missed".

B. TARGET MALFUNCTION

1. A target which breaks at launching shall be called a "no bird" and shooter will be provided a new target.

2. A target which is launched in an obviously different trajectory shall be called a "no bird" and the shooter will be provided a new target.

3. If a bad target or "no bird" is thrown on the second target of a double, and if the shooter has already attempted the first target prior to the Field Judges' call, the

attempt on the first target will be recorded as fired. The complete double will be repeated, however, the first target of the pair will remain as scored and the "proof double" will be thrown only to record the attempt on the second target. The shooter must make an attempt at both targets. Failure to make a legitimate attempt on the first target shall be cause for scoring the second target as "lost".

4. If a bad target or "no bird" is thrown during a timed reload sequence, the shooter will repeat the sequence beginning with the last target established.

As in the proof double described in VI-B-3 the shooter must make an attempt at the established target before proceeding with the remaining sequence. If the last established target occurred before the timed reload, the shooter shall begin the sequence accordingly and proceed through the reloading again. The Field Judge shall enforce his judgment (either by implementing a suitable penalty, or allowing a repeat of the reloading sequence) to prevent a "no bird" or "bad target" thrown after either a successful or an unsuccessful reloading attempt from changing the results of the initial sequence.

5. At a station of multiple targets, at least two good targets must be presented or a "no bird" will be called and the multiple targets will be attempted again. Multiple targets shall be shot as "fair in the air", two new shots will be attempted and scored, no scores from previous "no bird" attempts will stand.

6. Any targets broken by another target, or pieces from another target, will be called a "no bird" and treated as per paragraph VI-B-3.

VII. PROTESTS

A. A shooter may protest if in his opinion the rules as stated herein are improperly applied.

B. There will be no protests concerning calls or scoring of hits, or misses. The Field Judges final decision will stand.

C. Protests shall be made immediately upon completion of the shooting at a given field. Protest shall be made to the Shoot Official(s).

D. The Shoot Official(s) shall convene a predetermined "jury" of 3 to 5 Field Judges or competitors who are known to be representative of the shooters present and knowledgeable about these rules. The jury will decide on the validity of the protest and the resolution of the case. They will prescribe penalties or award bonuses as they determine to be fair and in the spirit of the competition.

VIII. MISCELLANEOUS

A. Safety is everyones responsibility.

B. It is the shooters responsibility to report any unsafe shooting condition immediately to Shoot Officials.

C. Stations at which the shooter is walking, setting in a blind and/or a boat or any other situation other than the regular standing position is not recommended. These stands all represent a simulated hunting situation; however, large crowds are not present during this type of hunting. Safety is the number one consideration for all Sporting Clays Ranges.

D. Shooters must have the direct permission of a Field Judge to test fire any gun. Other than on such permitted test firings, guns will be discharged only in attempt at competition targets.

E. Field Judges may be assisted by markers to record scores on the shooters' score cards.

F. It is the sole responsibility of the shooter to begin any event, station, and/or field with sufficient equipment and ammunition. Failure to do so, which in the opinion of the Field Judges will delay the shoot, will result in the loss of all targets as required to keep the shoot moving. Make-up targets will be provided only at the discretion of the shoot officials.

G. Formats for shootoffs to break ties shall be at the discretion of the Shoot Officials.

LEWIS CLASS

This system has been in common use for a good many years as a method of dividing optional money. It is also popular in a good many sections of the country as a means of distributing prizes where the past averages or known abilities of shooters are not available.

This system is based on the final scores as they are posted when the shoot has been completed and gives every contestant an equal chance to win, no matter what his shooting ability.

REMINDER: Classification has nothing to do with your "class" in the Lewis Class. Your class for this Event will be determined solely by the rules below.

When all the shooting has been completed, the scores are listed in numerical order from the highest to the lowest. They are then divided into as many groups as there are classes. For example, if there were 60 entries and 4 classes, there would be 15 scores in each class. The highest score in each class would then be the winner.

Since there will often be odd numbers of entries and tie scores on the dividing line between the classes, the following rules have been established:

1. Where a short class is necessary, due to odd entry list, the short class or classes shall head the list.

2. Where the line of division falls in a number of tie scores, the contestants are assigned to the class in which the majority of the scores appear.

3. Where an equal number of tie scores appear on either side of the line, contestants shall be assigned to the head of the lower class.

4. Where the original division is changed, due to tie scores, this change shall apply only to the classes directly affected and the original division shall continue in the other classes.

To cite an example, we will take a shoot containing a 200 target program in which there are 4 Lewis classes and 62 contestants. Since the short classes are placed first, there would be 15 shooters in Class 1 and 2 and 16 shooters in Classes 3 and 4. The final scores are arranged from highest to lowest and the lines drawn in between the classes.

Brackets represent assignment of scores according to Rules 2 and 3.
Horizontal lines represent division of all entries into classes according to Rule 1.

Class 1
180 Winner Class 1
179
179
178
178
178
178
177
177
177
176
175
175
174
174

Class 2
173 ⎱ 173's Tie
173 ⎰ for Class 2
172
170
170
169
168
167
167
167
165
164
163
163
163
—
163

Class 3
162 ⎫
162 ⎪
162 ⎬
162 ⎪
162 ⎭
161
161
160
159
158
157
157
157
157

Rule 2 places all
163's in Class 2
therefore 162's tie
for Class 3.

Class 4
156 ⎫
— ⎬
156 ⎭
154
153
150
149
149
148
147
146
145
144
144
140
140
139
135

Rule 3 places all 156's
in Class 4 and they are
tied for this Class